NEVER BETTER

NEVER BETTER

TWO KIDS, THEIR DAD, AND HIS WIFE'S GHOST

GONZALO RIEDEL

DUNDURN PRESS

Publisher: Kwame Scott Fraser | Acquiring editor: Julie Mannell | Editor: Susan Fitzgerald
Cover designer: Laura Boyle
Cover image: istock.com/Jesper Dickell

Library and Archives Canada Cataloguing in Publication

Title: Never better : two kids, their dad, and his wife's ghost / Gonzalo Riedel.
Names: Riedel, Gonzalo, author.
Identifiers: Canadiana (print) 20230520812 | Canadiana (ebook) 20230520820 | ISBN 9781459750395 (softcover) | ISBN 9781459750401 (PDF) | ISBN 9781459750418 (EPUB)
Subjects: LCSH: Riedel, Gonzalo—Family. | LCSH: Widowers—Canada—Biography. | LCSH: Cancer—Patients—Canada—Biography. | LCSH: Wives—Canada—Death—Biography. | LCGFT: Autobiographies.
Classification: LCC HQ1058.5.C3 R54 2024 | DDC 306.88/2092—dc23

We acknowledge the support of the Canada Council for the Arts and the Ontario Arts Council for our publishing program. We also acknowledge the financial support of the Government of Ontario, through the Ontario Book Publishing Tax Credit and Ontario Creates, and the Government of Canada.

Printed and bound in Canada.

Dundurn Press
1382 Queen Street East
Toronto, Ontario, Canada M4L 1C9
dundurn.com, @dundurnpress

For my kids.
Charlie. Deep breath in.
Elliot. Deep breath out.

MY WIFE, ERICA, could be fond of a sappy story. A tear-jerker.

I might have found this one a little clichéd, but she would have appreciated it.

High-school sweethearts. Boyfriend and girlfriend from down the way.

From the same neighbourhood, actually. Knew her back in kindergarten.

Would you believe I actually had a crush on her in kindergarten? The feeling wasn't reciprocated, that much I know. I'm not sure she would have even remembered me, had she not looked back through old school photos and seen me as child. She couldn't deny I was in her class, because there I was in her classroom photo. But what did she remember about me? I don't know.

You'd have to ask her.

That is, if you could. If she was around.

We met up again in high school. That old crush came back, but with hormonal high-school intensity. I was smitten with her again in a whole new way.

Again, I don't think she was particularly impressed. I was a pretty obnoxious kid. But I played the long game. I got in good with her circle of friends.

It was a good circle, honestly. We're all still friends. So it wasn't just some ruse.

But ahhh, my feelings got out. I blurted out something to one of my friends, and that friend blabbed, and it got around to Erica, which was embarrassing at the time.

But, hey. It all worked out. We got married. Had kids.

Then, uh-oh. She gets sick.

Really sick.

That's a story Erica would have eaten up. I'd have busted her chops about it.

"You gonna watch your sad terminal-illness movie?" I might have said offhandedly.

She'd be on the couch, blanket over her lap — the pink blanket that only felt nice on one side, the side that didn't pick up all the lint. Maybe she'd have a bowl of popcorn or crackers at the ready. "You don't have to watch it if you don't want to." That's what I imagine her saying. "Sometimes it just feels good to feel sad." That is something she almost certainly would have said.

I'd have scoffed. Maybe I'd have watched. But I probably wouldn't.

Cancer stories have never been my thing. I find them depressing.

° ° ° ° ° ° ° ° °

WE HAD TWO boys together. Elliot and then Charlie, three years later. Not even Charles. Just Charlie. They're ten and seven now.

Sometimes, I tell them stories about their mom. They used to come up a lot, because it was important that we remember. Stories still come up, but the sadness around the stories has mostly gone. There's a lightness to these stories now, a lack of urgency. When I do tell them things about their mom, I need them to understand a few caveats:

1. She isn't here to defend herself. Not that she's the type of person who needed defending. She rarely made herself a fool, or came away from a scenario looking like the bad guy. But these are the stories we like best about people. Ones that humanize us, or that create a sense of drama. I could tell them that she and I liked driving around and going thrift-store shopping and watching movies and being in each other's presence, but those sorts of stories rarely make for engaging narratives.

2. Not only is she not here to defend herself, she also isn't here to correct me on the details. I tend to forget timelines, to conflate incidences. When she and I would relay stories to friends, she was always correcting me on the things I'd gotten wrong. She'd remind me, "No, that didn't happen on that day," or "We were living at whatever apartment when that occurred," forcing me to acknowledge that my memory is a sham and that every true story I tell is made into fiction by accident.

3. This is probably the most important thing I tell them: As much as I want to tell stories about her and the things she did, the way she was, it's all filtered through my memories. It all exists in the way I see things, the effect it had on me, and the ways in which those memories have stayed with me.

Any story I tell about Erica is really a story about me. It's about the way she responded to my jokes, or the things she said that left an impression on me. My feelings about her.

I have to remind the kids that every story I tell about her is really about my relationship with her, and that getting to know her through my stories is to get to know me better.

They say that people are never really gone as long as they're remembered, and that by talking about the person, you keep them alive through memory. But maybe it's more about keeping ourselves alive. When a person dies, those memories you share together, they're half gone. It's up to you to remember them.

It's up to other people to remember them when you are gone.

When you die, and your memories have vanished into the ether, you have to ask: Did the things that happened in your life actually happen?

When you try to remember your past, and it's fuzzy, and you're unsure of the timeline or the order of events, how can you be sure what you experienced is real?

Of course, I don't say all this to my children. I still have the decency to rein it in a bit. I don't want them to develop a complex or anything.

o o o o o o o o

AT A CERTAIN point, you learn to guide a person's response when you tell them that your wife is dead. That even at your relatively young age, you're a widower. It comes up in conversation more than you'd think. Even when you don't want to talk about it, it's there. It's the foundation by which you live.

Let's say you're on a date. You've lived long enough in solitude and you're ready to go out and re-experience life.

She asks you about your kids, because you've mentioned them in conversation. She says, "Do you and their mom share custody?" It's implied that you two have separated. And that's true, in a manner of speaking.

You say, "No, their mom is deceased."

You've chosen those words carefully. It isn't "your wife," but "their mom." Even though you still see her as your wife, because you've never broken up, but you want to suggest distance. Personal growth. You aren't hung up on her anymore. You aren't married to a ghost.

"Deceased" is also a good word. It's clinical but not entirely informal. "She's dead" comes across as blunt. "Passed on" is vague, and it requires the listener just a moment to work through the euphemism. But "deceased" is emphatic.

"Oh," they say when you've told them. Usually, a person will screw up their face for a moment. Sometimes it's genuine and sometimes it isn't. There is always something performative about these moments, both for me and for the person receiving this information.

"That's awful," they say. "I'm so sorry to hear that."

You put your hands out so that you're showing your palms.

As if to say, "I know. I know."

What you actually say is, "Thank you."

You say, "It was a long time ago."

Your timing is precise.

You've said this before. Dozens of times. You've conveyed this information to others in different ways. This way is always the smoothest, the least difficult for you. The easiest for the person to process.

There is a negotiation at play.

The person you're speaking to will try to convey that they are willing to hear your story, as much as you want to tell it. But they do not want to overburden you. They know that this may not be the time or place to discuss matters of grief and mortality.

And you? You just don't want to kill the vibe.

So you allow a moment to pass, to let the sombreness run its course. You don't want to crack a joke too soon.

But you do want to crack a joke eventually.

"I guess this way I can have hot widower vibes," you say. "Like in an old gothic romance novel."

Your date smiles at this.

You say, "All I need now is a dusty old manor on the moors. With a double-wide staircase. And portraits of my ancestors painted onto velvet canvasses, where the eyes move when you walk across the room."

Or something.

You've addressed it. And now you're free to move on.

At least for right now.

Free to move on.

∘ ∘ ∘ ∘ ∘ ∘ ∘ ∘ ∘

AT SOME POINT during our high-school friendship, as I said, it became known that I had a crush on Erica. I told a friend who told a friend who told her. It certainly wouldn't have been me who told her this. I was too chickenshit at the time to make something like that clear.

She didn't see me in that romantic way. We were both young, and I don't think dating was much of a priority to her then. But, as it happens sometimes when you find out someone has a crush on you, you begin to see them in a new way. I was unaware this was happening to her. While I was trying to expand my social circle and date outside my friend group, Erica was quietly developing a crush on me.

Somehow, it came to a head one weekday evening, like a Tuesday or a Wednesday, when I was hanging out with a friend at my house and Erica was hanging out at another friend's house. It was like one of those Technicolor musicals where the screen gets split in two. On one side there's me being coerced into asking her out, and on the other side there's Erica being coerced into asking me out. It was all terribly juvenile, I'm sure, but that didn't make the emotions any less real. I was terrified of making myself vulnerable but was just as terrified of disrupting our friend circle at school. I'd have to spend a significant amount of time with her in class for the remainder of that year, and probably through high school. The last thing I needed was to feel embarrassed that whole time.

But there I was, gathering up the courage to call her.

"Do it," my friend said. "I hear she'll say yes."

"I don't know ..." I said. This all seemed like a big put-on. Like I was being set up for failure and mockery.

"Don't be a coward."

"Fine," I said.

Next thing I knew, my friend had dialed the number and handed me the receiver.

"Hello," I said, gritting my teeth. Pretending I was too cool to be scared. "Is Erica there?"

I could hear her friend stifle a giggle. "She sure is," she said, passing the phone.

"Hello?" Erica said.

I skipped the general pleasantries and all that. There was a task at hand, and I needed to get to it before the fear could catch up to me.

"Hi, Erica," I said. "Um, hey. Do you want to go out some time?"

"Uh, okay," she said. "Yes."

"Huh." A huge wave of relief came over me. She said yes? Holy smokes, she said yes! "Okay! Awesome!" In the background I could hear her friends quietly cheering her on. Erica and I both laughed.

"Well," I said, "I'll see you at school tomorrow!"

Having got what I wanted, I hung up before having the chance to make a fool of myself.

"There," I said to my friend. "That wasn't so hard."

◦ ◦ ◦ ◦ ◦ ◦ ◦ ◦

I CAN UNDERSTAND how it might seem like I'm taking apart my wife, who was once flesh and blood and very much alive, breaking her down into pieces and then re-assembling her like stripped car parts into little more than anecdotes and plot devices. It might seem exploitative, or ghoulish.

Imagine how I feel about it.

◦ ◦ ◦ ◦ ◦ ◦ ◦ ◦

OUR EARLY DATES were so naive. We took walks around the neighbourhood. Went to movies. Went thrift-store shopping.

Actually, those all sound pretty fun, even now.

I was always trying to move a little too fast for her. I wanted to hold hands and make out well before she was ready. She was a shy kisser, and we went out for months before even trying that.

It's understandable. We were new to this.

◦ ◦ ◦ ◦ ◦ ◦ ◦ ◦

BEING THE LAST parent alive puts a certain pressure on a person. I used to be a risk-taker. When I was eighteen, I hitchhiked halfway across Canada, from Winnipeg to Vancouver, for the fun of it. The next year I went out east, from Winnipeg to Montreal. My mom was worried about me for obvious reasons, scared I'd be murdered and mutilated, left on the side of the road. She made me promise to stick to the Trans-Canada Highway, which spans the country, end to end, so that I might leave a traceable path. I can't imagine doing a thing like that now, hitching rides with strangers, just like I can't imagine skydiving, bungee jumping, or any other sport with a high risk of orphaning my children.

A few months ago, I slipped on some stairs and suffered a nasty landing. Not many stairs, just a few. The kids were playing at a neighbour's house across the street, and I had just baked an apricot crumble. It was a rainy afternoon, and something warm and sugary felt like an appropriate way of thanking my neighbours for watching the kids and giving me a few free hours.

I stepped out onto the stairs descending from my front door, and my foot slipped on the wet wood. It felt exaggerated and cartoonish, like something out of Bugs Bunny. I protected the ceramic dish and not my body. My upper spine took the brunt of the fall.

We've all fallen before, but this was different. The sensation was something new. I panicked, convinced that I'd done forever-type damage to myself. Immediately, I imagined my kids adjusting to a life where their father could no longer walk. I looked across to the neighbours' house, hoping someone had caught sight of this brutal fall, that someone would come to my rescue. I called for help, but the impact had winded me so badly that my words came out in ugly grunts, like the bark of an injured seal. The apricot crumble looked unharmed, but it was getting drizzled on.

Luckily, someone did spot the fall, and he and his son rushed over to help. The man asked if I had hit my head. No, thank God. This was a new thought to panic over. He wanted to know if I could move my toes. I was pretty sure I felt them move inside my shoes. He tried to raise me to my feet, but I waved him away for the time being so I could move on my own time.

I pointed to the dessert dish. "Can you bring that inside out of the rain?" It came out a wheeze.

The teenager put two optimistic thumbs up. "Hopefully, you don't have to go to the hospital," he chimed. His father glared at him. "What?" the boy asked.

"Seemed a little insensitive," his dad said.

I groaned and coughed. "I have to say ..." It was a labour to get anything out. "I have to say I agree with your father."

The rest of the day, I was something of an emotional wreck, often bursting into tears in front of the kids. I'd try to organize a comfortable position on the floor, a yoga mat offering the barest of support, but any slight shift in my upper back or movement in my shoulders would make my body scream at me for having dared to move. I replayed the fall in my mind, and each time I came closer and closer to hitting my head. I was *this close* to dying on those stairs. Or maybe I wasn't.

"Please take it easy on me," I told the kids, my eyes dampening. "Daddy's in a lot of pain."

∘ ∘ ∘ ∘ ∘ ∘ ∘ ∘ ∘ ∘

THERE IS A scar between my eyes from a cereal bowl. I was unloading the clean dishes from the dishwasher in our old apartment, and I noticed some hardened oatmeal stuck to the bowl. Having gone through the hot wash and then the drying cycle, it was more like concrete.

I chipped away at the formation with my thumbnail, grinding it down as best I could. My thumb slipped off the bowl, and the bowl snapped back like an elastic. Into my face. The dull rim of a ceramic IKEA bowl hit me between the eyes, and I bled like an old-time wrestler. You can still see the mark.

This is all to say, I don't rely on my wits alone to keep me alive.

° ° ° ° ° ° ° °

ERICA AND I dated steadily into our twenties before we moved in together, but until then we each lived with our parents. We would drive around, looking for quiet places to fool around. We may not have had a lovers' lane, but we did have industrial parks and hidden parking lots. I have no idea what went on inside the buildings, but I have first-hand knowledge of what happened outside them.

We would fool around in the back seat, fogging up the windows, and when another car would drive by, we'd stop moving and slump down low, pretending like nothing was going on. Like this was some normal, erratically parked car behind some building, next to the garbage bins.

One time a car pulled up outside our parked car, and some angry, burly dude got out and banged on my window.

"What are you doing to my sister?" he shouted at me.

As if he didn't know.

Erica had shielded her face from him up to that point. Then she looked right at him. Erica didn't have any brothers.

The man recognized his error and threw his hands up in the universal sign of apology. I have no idea where his actual sister was. Neither did he, clearly. Probably in another parking lot somewhere. He backed away to his car.

"My mistake," he said.

I thought this was the funniest thing to happen all week, but Erica was horrified, so we didn't get to finish up.

◦ ◦ ◦ ◦ ◦ ◦ ◦ ◦ ◦

EVER SINCE THE kids were babies, I dreamed of the day they'd be adults. They'd have their own friends, their own hustles. Maybe they'd have girlfriends or boyfriends of their own, back aches, student loans.

I imagined myself turning to them with so much sober gravitas, and saying, "Hey, guess what? I totally had sex with your mom."

It just wouldn't be funny now.

◦ ◦ ◦ ◦ ◦ ◦ ◦ ◦ ◦

I THINK ABOUT what it'd be like for her if I had died instead. Would she find herself on a dating site? With the horror stories I've heard from women, I can only wonder at the calibre of creep who would talk to her.

I picture her on dates, having flings, feeling heartbreak. I get jealous at these thoughts, but not in the way I would be if we separated. I'm not jealous of the men in these scenarios, the ones in her life instead of me. I'm jealous of *her*, because she gets to stay behind and live, and I don't because I'm dead.

○ ○ ○ ○ ○ ○ ○ ○

ELLIOT AND CHARLIE come from a line of single parents.

My father left us when I was seven, and my mom raised me and my brothers, Pablo and Rodrigo. They were twelve and seventeen when he left.

My parents manoeuvred things behind my back. I don't blame them, on account of my being seven. I don't know exactly what my brothers knew while it was happening, or if they only understood the details years later.

We went to Chile over Christmas and New Year's, at the end of the 1980s. My parents grew up in Chile. They escaped a hairy political climate in the 1970s and moved to Canada with Rodrigo, who was the only one born at the time.

When I say we went to Chile, I don't mean to say we went together. We travelled in two separate groups, for reasons that were not clearly explained to me then. Pablo and I went with our mom, and Rodrigo and my dad travelled together on a separate itinerary. They'd be a week behind us, was what I was told.

So we returned to Winnipeg sometime in January, Pablo and my mom and me. My dad and Rodrigo were due to follow us there a week later, but Rodrigo flew back alone. My dad stayed behind. He'd be back soon, I was told.

Within a few days, my mom broke the news to me. I had been playing by myself in the backyard, building paths and structures in the snow. When I came inside, my mom was sitting on a chair in the middle of the kitchen. I supposed she hadn't wanted to sit under the bright kitchen light, so she'd turned on the hallway light instead, and it cast a discomforting, eerie glow in the room, full of long shadows. She had been bracing herself to have this conversation. I remember she sat rigid and tense.

"I have to talk to you about something," she said.

I removed my snow-covered boots and went to her.

She took a deep breath and laid it out as clearly as she could.

"It's about your father," she said. "He isn't coming home."

"What?" I could feel my stomach dropping through the floor.

"He has decided to stay in Chile to live there."

That was all it took for everything to change. A couple of sentences. Then the world was different.

That would happen to me a few more times in life. It happens to all of us.

I can only imagine how my mom was feeling when she told me. How she must have rehearsed the words in her head before I came inside.

I had to do the same thing once as an adult. Tell Elliot that his mom wasn't coming home.

° ° ° ° ° ° ° ° °

ERICA AND I didn't move in together until our early twenties. She was ready to make the jump from her parents' place before I was, and it wasn't until she began looking for apartments in earnest that I decided to make the jump too. She had planned on rooming with a friend, and when that fell through I took it as a sign to grow up and move out with her.

Our first apartment was roughly the size of a utility closet. The building was about a hundred years old, and it was run by a caretaker named Edith who was born around the time they laid the foundations. She was ninety-three, and she was insistent on still doing her job in her golden years. I hope it was for a sense of purpose, and not financial necessity. She had an English accent like the teapot in *Beauty and the Beast.*

After living there for a time, I noticed that deep below our kitchen sink, the pipes were emitting an ominous bubbling that suggested something might explode and erupt. I reported the problem to Edith.

"The building just does that," she said, shooing the problem away with a dismissive wave. "I just say the building gets the gurgledy-burgledies."

The day we moved in, Erica had to work through the afternoon while I loaded boxes into the apartment, and I had to be at work in the evening when she came home. When we weren't going to school, she worked at a shoe store in the mall and I was at a pizza place, the same one I had worked at since I was sixteen. She'd expected me to unpack at least *some* of the boxes. But I wasn't a particularly motivated person. I'd only opened one box, the one with the cutlery, so I could dig out a large spoon and then use that spoon to scoop a heroic dollop of ice cream into my mouth. Then I'd run a bath for myself and smoked a joint, leaving the unsmoked half on the rim of the tub. Erica didn't need to be a forensic investigator to trace the events that took place before her arrival. When I came home from my own shift, she had only just finished unpacking the boxes, and she was pretty annoyed at having done all of it on her own. She'd been expecting to come home to a fair amount of work, but not like this. It was our first apartment in what was to be a partnership, and I had set the bar super low.

∘ ∘ ∘ ∘ ∘ ∘ ∘ ∘ ∘

SHE WAS A great audience for my jokes. I miss that as much as anything — hearing her laugh. I chased that sound, the timbre of a good giggle. It was meditative, like wind chimes.

But when a joke horrified her, her mouth made the most perfectly shocked O. I was young and insensitive and willing to cross any line to get that reaction.

Sometimes when I imagine the alternate-universe scenario, where I died and she lived, I become fiercely jealous of some guy coming along and getting those laughs. Sorry, fictional dating app guy, you can't have those laughs. They're mine.

∘ ∘ ∘ ∘ ∘ ∘ ∘ ∘ ∘

THOSE FIRST FEW years living together were pretty fun, once we'd established our space. Not only was the apartment absurdly small, but the window separating the den from the bedroom had been knocked out some time before we'd moved in. I would stay up late after my work shift watching movies after she went to bed, and the sound and lights often kept her awake. I often left dirty socks and dishes scattered about the floor. I guess I should say living there was fun for me, and probably a pain in the ass for her.

It must not have been too bad for her, though, because when our lease expired we moved into a bigger apartment, in the basement just beneath us. We toted our junk and our cat down the stairs, and suddenly we had room to manoeuvre.

We cooked dinners, watched TV, cracked jokes, had sex, enjoyed each other's company whenever our schedules aligned. We didn't have to live for anyone else. It was okay to be selfish when we wanted to be. We were only responsible to ourselves.

∘ ∘ ∘ ∘ ∘ ∘ ∘ ∘

ERICA WANTED HER great-grandmother's engagement ring as her own. She clued me in to how much new engagement rings were meant to cost, and I blessed that woman for her thriftiness and sentimentality. I knew she wanted that ring because she had told me several times, making sure she was clear. "My parents have it. So get it off them."

So I did. And I did it old-fashioned like. I asked for their blessings.

They kind of laughed at the sincerity of it, because they hadn't known me to be especially sincere. I could tell they appreciated the gesture.

Her mom brought out the engagement ring for me.

I also told them that I didn't know when and how I'd ask her to marry me. I would care for the ring until I felt the time was right, and I'd ask her when I was ready. I asked them to please not let on to Erica that I had the ring.

It had to be a worthwhile proposal. Including our high-school years, we'd been dating for the better part of a decade, and we now lived together. Erica would be mad at me if I half-assed the proposal.

Maybe a month or two passed. We had planned a camping trip. We loved camping together. I made sure we booked a campsite that looked out over the water. I asked if she'd bring that summer dress that she looked good in, which might have been an early tip-off for her. But I felt she appreciated a pleasant aesthetic. She wouldn't want to be wearing a baggy sweatshirt in her engagement story. I just knew she wouldn't.

I had a vision for it. Tent set up. Early evening fire crackling. Sunset over the water. Both of us looking our outdoor best.

The day before we left for the trip, I was awoken by a phone call from her mom. I had been working late nights, and I was half asleep.

"Is Erica there?" she asked.

I croaked, "No. She's at work."

"Oh. Did I wake you?"

"Yeah."

She said, "You gonna ask her this weekend?"

"Yeah."

"Okay. Good luck."

I went back to sleep.

Another tip-off came on our way out to Rushing River. That's where we were headed. I kept commenting on how I hoped there was a nice sunset that night, and how I'd wanted to hurry to have the camp set up by sunset.

"You kept saying sunset, sunset," she told me afterward.

We assembled the tent and loaded it up with our inflatable bedding. She stayed inside the tent to organize it while I stepped out to start a fire. Just a small one. Less for warmth and more to pepper the air with smoke.

When Erica emerged from the tent, she was wearing the summer dress. The one I liked. She poured herself a drink and sat down on a felled log that had been smoothed over time into a seat. I climbed into the tent to change my own clothes into something more presentable. No sense proposing to her looking ragged.

I wasn't worried she'd say no. The thought never crossed my mind. But still, I was terrified in that moment, shaking, trying to throw on a button-down shirt inside a tent at Rushing River.

I stepped out. There she was. My girlfriend. Soon-to-be fiancée. Pretty as can be.

I had something planned. Some sort of flowery preamble about how much she meant to me, and how she made me feel when we were together. Something articulate. Whatever I had planned to say didn't matter. A jumble of words tumbled out my mouth. Utter nonsense, probably.

Despite my earlier tells, the proposal still came as a genuine shock to her. When I dropped to a knee, she blurted out, "What are you doing?" And when I brought out the box with the ring, her great-grandmother's ring, her hands flew over her mouth in surprise. I'd even had it resized for her, using a ring she already wore as reference.

"Erica," I said, "will you marry me?"

Hell, yeah. I absolutely nailed that proposal.

° ° ° ° ° ° ° °

THERE'S A LITTLE stuffed tiger on Charlie's bed that he must have discovered around the house. I bought it back when Erica and I were still dating, and we had been for a long while. By this time Erica was becoming anxious for a wedding proposal, and she had somehow convinced herself that I was going to propose to her over Christmas. After all, she loved Christmas, and I had been hinting that this year's present was going to be a good one.

Well, she was wrong. I wasn't planning to propose to her at all that Christmas. I got her a record player, because she'd hinted she wanted one, and some records by her favourite artists. I thought it was a good gift.

The stuffed tiger was also one of the gifts. Even into adulthood she was a sucker for filling her bed with stuffed toys, and I thought she'd like it. She was fond of kitschy cute things like this tiger, with its disproportionately large head and its huge marble eyes. I stuffed it into a tiny box and wrapped it up. It was a small tiger, and the tiny box I'd crammed it into looked roughly the size of a jewellery box, from Erica's perspective.

Well, I didn't find out until later — until after I'd actually proposed — that she'd opened that box expecting something more than a six-dollar stuffed tiger. She was keeping it stored in a box, which was unlike her, and I asked if she didn't like it. Only then did she give me her perspective on my Christmas gift that year. "I thought it was going to be an engagement ring," she told me, "but it was just that goddamned tiger."

∘ ∘ ∘ ∘ ∘ ∘ ∘ ∘ ∘

SOME THINGS THAT drove me batty about Erica:

- When she came home from shopping, she had to show me every single thing that she'd bought. Every. Single. Thing. It was the same when she showed me photos. "Show me your best three or four film rolls," I would tell her. "After that I'm checked out."
- She talked when I watched *Jeopardy!* Not during the commercials or the interview parts,

oh no. She would say nothing until gameplay and then chatter over the questions.

- She had this dumb pink blanket that was more cat hair and lint than fabric. Whenever you felt something lumpy and uncomfortable on the couch, underneath your butt, it was the blanket.
- She didn't like to dance. It made her feel embarrassed, even in the privacy of our house.
- She hated cilantro.

Look, I know this list really just makes me look like a grouch. Maybe that's the case. Maybe the problem wasn't her dumb blanket at all. I wish I could do it again, and really appreciate the things that annoyed me.

∘ ∘ ∘ ∘ ∘ ∘ ∘ ∘ ∘

HERE'S A LIST I'm sure she'd have made about me if things were reversed. Things about Gonzalo that irritated Erica:

- He never stopped quoting old *Simpsons* episodes, no matter how inappropriate the timing.
- He would always leave his socks and underwear on the floor, and he never closed drawers completely. They'd always be overstuffed, and things would stick out everywhere.
- He would tell the same stories over and over, no matter how many times his suffering wife had to hear them.
- His taste in music was one-quarter let's call it "arty." *Some* of it was good.

- He would go out for late-night walks and stay out for hours, coming home reeking of cigarettes.
- He would never tidy unless the mess was past a tipping point where he would have to clean or else lose his sanity, and then he would rest on his laurels for weeks, bragging about when he cleaned a single room that one time.
- He spent all of his paycheque immediately, and on stupid things, and then he would be endlessly critical of spending his money on important things, like going out, or getting Christmas gifts.
- He was maybe *too* good at kissing.

○ ○ ○ ○ ○ ○ ○ ○ ○

I WORRY ABOUT how I'm representing Erica. What if I'm not capturing who she is. Is that important? Can I remember who she is, or do I only remember some idealized version of her? I want to show her for who she was, but it's an uncomfortable thing giving her dialogue in this book. I'm literally putting words into her mouth. What I loved about her is that she wouldn't have stood for me putting words into her mouth.

○ ○ ○ ○ ○ ○ ○ ○ ○

JUST RELAX, GUY. Don't take it too much to heart.

It's just your dead wife's legacy. A written document of the generational trauma you're passing on to your children.

No pressure.

∘ ∘ ∘ ∘ ∘ ∘ ∘ ∘ ∘

ERICA ARRANGED A fairly lavish wedding on the cheap. That was a skill of hers. She came of age during a glut of do-it-yourself–themed renovation shows on TV, admiring the thrifty, make-do approach these people had. She'd rather have lived by her wits than with money, which was for the best because we never had any.

At first we looked into renting a church for the ceremony. She wanted to appease some more devout family members by keeping some religion in it. Also, Erica herself wanted to keep a bit of the God stuff. I could take it or leave it. It didn't work out, in any case, because of the church's booking schedule.

We settled on an outdoor sculpture garden for the ceremony, and added a smidge of God in the ceremony script. The rental cost ate up most of the meagre budget, but it was worth it. A sculpture garden in the springtime is every bit as charming and colourful as you'd expect. Guests walked through the winding, flower-lined path to a cordoned-off section in the back, reserved for private functions like ours.

For the reception, we reserved the upstairs of a pub we all liked. Since then it's been renovated into something unrecognizable, but back then the tables and booths were old oak things that had experienced their share of spilled whiskey and stale cigarette smoke. We hired a DJ to play Motown soul music.

Erica made the cake herself. A three-tiered cake patterned black with pink polka dots, like an Audrey Hepburn cocktail dress. Her wedding gown cost next to nothing too — she'd repurposed her grandmother's wedding dress. She even made the centrepieces for the tables herself.

Somehow, we'd been in possession of a book of golden-age–era Hollywood movie posters. She bought a dozen or so clear, circular vases from the dollar store, lined them each with a movie poster, weighed them with aesthetically pleasing stones, and placed a fake flower inside. At the end of the night, friends scouted these out as keepsakes, and I've seen a few at friends' houses still. She even got me into the spirit. She offered me the task of curating a mix CD for everyone as a gift. She had a few requests to include, and we together had some personal songs that reminded us of one another, and she printed out lovely CD labels of a pink daisy with our wedding date on it.

In all, she organized the heck out of that wedding.

One of my favourite memories was after we left, when we got home.

No, I'm not talking about that, you scoundrels.

But yeah, that was fun.

After that, I mean, hanging out in lazy clothes on the living room floor. Still a little bit drunk, but not as drunk as you might think. We were opening up the wedding cards that were filled with money.

Hey, we were poor. It was only right to accept our gifts with eagerness.

My former boss from my old pizza-place job, who we'd invited, gave us a card with a stack of cash and a joint rolled up with it.

People told me the wedding day goes by fast. A lot happens, but it goes quick. It certainly did. But it's the stuff afterward I remember best. Erica and me, cross-legged on the living room floor, smoking a joint we'd been given as a wedding gift, reading aloud these wonderful cards given to us by our favourite people, laughing and congratulating each other on being husband and wife. Comfortable with each other, absolutely in love.

What a time to be alive.

∘ ∘ ∘ ∘ ∘ ∘ ∘ ∘

WE MOVED TO Montreal after we got married, but before there were kids. We were in our mid-twenties. It had been twenty years since we met in kindergarten. Montreal was the place to go if you were an arty Winnipegger, bored and ready to explore somewhere new. An extended stay with an implied return. If you went east, to Toronto or Montreal, you tended to stay about two years, and we were no exception. People who went west to British Columbia fared better, and tended to stay away twice as long.

Officially, we went because I got into graduate school there. We had finished our undergraduate degrees, and I had a hankering to continue studying. We went to a predominantly French city so I could study English. It was my only application. The goal was to leave Winnipeg. I was too big for my britches. Erica didn't want to leave her friends and family for an extended period. But I was restless, and I wanted to go more than she wanted to stay.

She wasn't thrilled about moving. Winnipeg was our home, and she was restless to start a new chapter of our life, one that involved kids and a house. I think she saw those things as markers of adulthood. I guess I saw them as that too, and I wasn't ready. I told her when I was done my schooling, we could discuss children. It seemed to me the responsible decision. No one wants to raise a newborn while drafting a thesis. But it was also something of a cop-out. I wasn't serious about academics as much as it was something to do to push back the crushing weight of adulthood. I wasn't ready for kids or a mortgage or any of that stuff. I wanted to get drunk and catch the metro to cool loft parties with cheap beer and cigarettes.

It's still a lifestyle I endorse. It made Erica pretty lonely, though. For the first few months, she would work remotely from home, so she didn't have work colleagues to socialize with. Sometimes, she would come along to my grad school parties, but I think she felt out of place with my school friends, all of us with inside jokes and anecdotes about professors. She made do when she could, but usually she would stay home and watch TV under a blanket on the couch, alone, in a city she didn't really want to be in. I don't regret having gone to Montreal, or having been selfish about my youth, but had we known her time would be limited, that she could have spent those years closer to friends and family, with her own children, well, maybe we'd have chosen differently.

When my coursework had finished, we came back to Winnipeg for the same reason we'd left, only this time she wanted to come home more than I wanted to stay in Montreal. It was okay. I still had a thesis to focus on. Most of the friends I'd made in Montreal were now graduating and moving away to different cities. It felt like the last days of summer camp when the tents are packed up and the lush green leaves begin to show hints of yellow and red around the fringes.

∘ ∘ ∘ ∘ ∘ ∘ ∘ ∘

WE DISCUSSED HAVING children. She was ready for them. I was a coward.

I would find ways to prolong things, to move the goal posts.

We can't yet. Not while I'm in school.

Let me finish my thesis.

We'll get on our feet first. Let's be situated.

Every time she brought things up in concrete terms, I shut her down.

No. I didn't shut her down. I simply shut down. Refused to co-operate. But it was an act.

We compromised. I needed to first get comfortable enough to freefall. I explained it to her.

When I was in junior high, I'd try to jump off the top diving board at the swimming pool, but the board was too high for me. I'd look over the edge and chicken out. My knees would tremble. A shudder would run up my torso. If I could see it all, the full length of the pool, the distance to the water, the way the fluorescent light reflected the area beneath me, I'd become overwhelmed and have to step away.

So I stopped looking down to gauge my landing. I'd only look down to make sure nobody was swimming beneath me. I didn't want to clobber anyone from way up there.

I'd step away to gather my courage. Erase it all from my memory, the distance to the rippling water. I didn't need it to step off the diving board. All I needed was gravity, and just a moment of conviction.

I would walk over the edge, and only then would I look straight down. While plummeting, I'd take that one big breath. By then it was too late to go back.

"This is what I need to do," I told Erica. "I need to get comfortable enough to jump. And then I'll jump. Some time in a bit, I'll just tell you to stop taking your birth control pills. You'll ask, 'Are you sure?' I'll say yes. And then you won't say anything else because it might psych me out. But let's just be relaxed about it and have fun. I don't want to be that couple that schedules things on like an ovulation cycle or anything like that. If we start doing that, I might just chicken out again."

She asked, "Did you just compare jumping off a diving board at twelve to having a baby?"

"Do we have a deal?" I asked.

"They're barely even close," she said.

° ° ° ° ° ° ° °

I HAD A health scare in Montreal. The first big one that made me consider my own mortality. Before that I was invincible, too naive to ever consider it. Even when I was eighteen and I hitchhiked across the country, with the risk of being murdered and discarded by some deranged psychopath, I always believed myself impervious to real harm. It hadn't occurred to me that I was just a bag of meat, lined with clockwork that could be gummed up at any moment.

I had gone out drinking and dancing with some grad student friends. Drenched-in-sweat kind of dancing. We moved like we were on ecstasy. By the time I'd walked my friends home, the subways had stopped running, so I snoozed in the metro station until the sun came up and transit was back on schedule.

Throughout the night, a blood clot had formed behind my left shin, but I didn't know that. I could feel it when I woke up, and it caused me to limp around a bit. I could locate the affliction when I pressed my thumbs into my calf, and for an hour a dimple remained where the thumb had been. I thought it was just a sore muscle, or a minor sprain caused by the dancing, and I resumed my life.

But the pain increased, and so, too, did the swelling. I re-diagnosed my condition from a simple sprain to a torn muscle. I had been taking boxing classes, and I asked my coach what to do. He suggested ice and bed rest. Neither worked. The clot was damming up the blood flow through my leg, and everything south of the clot ballooned as the reservoir of blood pooled up.

After a few weeks, my leg had swollen to twice its size. When I wore shorts, people noticed the difference from across the road. More than that, the flesh had become soggy and bloated. Like it had been dragged from the river. Even still, once I finally checked myself into the hospital, I became impatient in the waiting room and nearly left without being checked out. A nurse specifically asked me to reconsider leaving, suspecting the diagnosis. When they confirmed the clot, doctors put me on a regimen of blood thinners, administered via pre-loaded syringes that I injected into the flab of my tummy.

Every time I returned to the clinic for a follow-up, I'd speak with a new doctor. They all scrutinized my blood tests and told me they couldn't find a cause for my clot. They asked me the same questions: Did I have a genetic history of deep vein thrombosis? Had I flown recently? Did I wear tight-fitting undergarments that could constrict my blood flow?

I noticed a pattern in these doctors that would repeat itself when Erica became sick. All these doctors were chasing the glory, trying to crack the mystery or solve the problem. It felt like a matter of competitive pride more than the desire to help. I suppose any motivator is better than no motivator.

The clot did eventually thin out and disappear. I guess the doctors got this one right.

° ° ° ° ° ° ° °

AT LAST, WE were on the same page about having children.

More or less.

Even if I was hesitant about dedicating myself to parenting, I knew nine months was a long time to get with the program.

Plus, I'd promised Erica that I'd commit myself to it when I was done school. I only needed to write my thesis. She'd waited long enough for me. We were back in Winnipeg, living in a new place. She knew what she wanted at this point in life, and I was just as content to let things pass me by.

Erica wanted kids more than I did, and I didn't want to hold her back. So hey, good for the bear.

When I was ready take the steps, I asked her, "How much is left on your birth control prescription?"

"About two weeks."

"Okay," I said. "Maybe ..." Deep breath. "Maybe when you're done those, you don't refill them."

She smiled. "You sure?"

"Yes. Let's not talk about this."

She got pregnant super quickly. She figured it happened the night we took a bottle of wine out onto the balcony.

I was working from home the day she told me. I got the news in almost real time. She came home and hurried into the bathroom. I figured she was just anxious to go. How should I have known she had taken a pregnancy test into the bathroom with her? When she came out, she tapped me on the shoulder so I'd take my headphones off. Work was making me a little cranky.

"Do you have a second?" she asked.

"Kind of. What is it?"

"Um. I'm pregnant?" She said it like a question.

For years I had imagined some scenario like this. I was worried I'd run my mouth and say the wrong thing, or that I would flub the moment in some way. I thought it best to say nothing at all for a minute, and to try acting stoic for once in my life. I stood up and gave her a huge hug. It was the right response, and it gave me a second to get my mind right.

"That's great news, babe."

She told me she'd thought of presenting me the news in some cutesy way, but given the circumstances, all she had on hand was the pregnancy test, and she didn't want to bring out the thing she'd peed on.

"Yes, I appreciate that," I said.

The rest of my work-from-home shift went more smoothly.

I was excited for the baby. Mostly. Sometimes.

I was excited when people asked me about the baby. Friends or family telling me how things were going to be now. I went along with it, smiling. But I was also wilfully ignorant of the baby's arrival. Erica's belly got bigger and I pretended nothing in our lives was changing. I'd go to coffee shops and pubs to finish writing my thesis. While Erica stayed home, I'd drink beer and flirt with strangers. It never went beyond that playful chatter, but it was disrespectful. It was shady.

I tried to be gentlemanly during her pregnancy. I rubbed her feet and arranged the pillows into something she might consider comfortable. She craved deli sandwiches but couldn't eat the meat due to a recent listeria scare in the processed meat industry. I steam-cooked slices of roast beef and got her the good rye bread and fancy mustard she liked.

At night I'd panic. I'd hang around the pub, flirting and drinking, a total wreck.

"Babies are easy," a friend told me. "They basically don't move for like a half a year, and by then you're better at parenting. Your skill level goes up when theirs does. They're basically house plants for a while. All you have to do is keep them alive."

I scanned the plants in our apartment. They'd all withered and gone brown.

At the seven- or eight-month mark, I started to take the baby's arrival seriously. I even looked forward to his arrival. Strangely, it never felt totally real. Even when he was in front of me. Even while I held him in my arms.

Only in brief glimmers did it dawn on me how things were different. I'd be doing dishes in the kitchen while Erica played with Elliot in the living room. I'd think, "Wow, this is our life. We have a kid." And the feeling would pass. Or we'd be in the car on a road trip, and I'd realize that, in this situation, I was the dad behind the wheel.

Me.

How the heck did this happen?

° ° ° ° ° ° ° °

"GET YOUR SLEEP now." This is a thing people sometimes say to you when a first baby is on its way. As if sleep can be banked like overtime hours.

"Are you going to be in the delivery room too?" asked one particularly tactless father.

I tell him it isn't the 1950s. "So yeah, probably."

"Man," he said, "it's going to be so gross. You see *everything*." He studied me with a lurid appraisal.

I couldn't tell what he was driving at. "I was there during the conception," I said. "I've already seen everything."

"Not like this," he told me.

His wife told him maybe to stop talking. "Maybe Gonzalo and Erica don't want to hear this," she said.

He leaned in. "Sometimes," he said, "sometimes there's shit. That's something they don't tell you. Women shit when they give birth."

The rest of us at the dinner table put down our forks.

∘ ∘ ∘ ∘ ∘ ∘ ∘ ∘ ∘

ERICA'S WATER BROKE and we rushed ourselves into a long wait at triage. Well, I rushed, because it's what I knew from television, but she had the sense to slow me down.

I was in the shower when she called to me from outside the curtain.

"Hon?"

"Yuh-huh."

"Um …"

I stuck my head out the shower curtain. "What's up?"

"I think my water broke."

"Oh, shit," I said. "I'll hurry!" It came out as a shout.

"Just calm down," she said. "There's no rush."

"Are you sure?"

"Yes. Finish your shower. I'm just going to sit down for a few minutes."

I was surprised how mundane the whole experience was. She wasn't having contractions yet, so they sent us home and told us to return later that day at a set time, or when contractions reached a certain frequency, whichever came first.

We returned to the hospital for our scheduled time and continued to wait around triage, hoping for her uterus to hurry it up already. Elliot was already a week overdue, and he would hold on for every available second. We scrolled our Facebook feeds and ate fried chicken.

The nurse asked Erica, "Would you like a Warm Judy Enema?"

"I'm sorry, what?"

"It's a trick I learned here," the nurse said. "I administer a Warm Judy Enema, and labour tends to start very shortly after. It's a good way to get the ball rolling."

"Are you Judy?" I asked.

"I am," Nurse Judy confirmed.

"Are you warm or is the enema warm?"

"The enema."

"Is this like a special patented type of enema?"

"Ha! It should be!" Judy flagged caught the attention of another nurse within earshot and suggested patenting it.

Erica hadn't a clue what to make of this proposition. "Should I do it?" she asked me. I could feel the fried chicken from earlier sitting in my gut like an undigested brick. I felt bloated and uncomfortable.

"I would absolutely do it," I said. "I don't see a single downside to it."

It took her some time to acquiesce, but at some point she went off with Room Temperature Judy to get herself shot full of warm enema.

Nurse Judy was absolutely full of it. The enema did nothing to speed up delivery. Things stagnated until the morning shift began and the doctors administered the Pitocin to get Erica's contractions going.

Somehow, I managed to be jealous of Erica. Not because it was her who got to experience the beauty of birthing something living into the world. No, gross.

I was jealous because my stomach still felt kind of awful. I wanted that enema.

° ° ° ° ° ° ° ° °

WE TOOK ELLIOT home to our apartment on the twenty-first floor. At times, the chandelier in that apartment would swing and sway as if being pushed around by ghosts, and we would realize that the building was rocking from the wind, but we couldn't feel it.

It was so tall that some days, when I stood on the balcony, I felt compelled to throw myself over the edge just to experience the sensation of falling. Never was it a suicidal urge, but even still, I imagined hoisting myself from a chair to the iron crossbeam and swan diving into the open air. Maybe parkour off the walls if I insisted on the less-graceful approach.

For a moment, the thrill of jumping would seem exhilarating, and I'd have to cross the threshold back into the apartment to settle my urge to toss myself over. I could imagine the surreal rush of falling, like my favourite carnival rides. Like a joy of an especially fast elevator. And then, as I'd plummet toward the concrete, to the stretch of loading zone next to the building's parking lot, I would already miss my family. My wife. My newborn child. And then a melancholy would sweep over me, even in the fantasy, and I'd lose the urge to jump.

° ° ° ° ° ° ° ° °

BABIES! THEY FALL asleep in the middle of eating and then wake up screaming. Sounds to me like a depression jag.

We managed to overcome our exhaustion the best we could while dealing with our lives being upended by this crying little poo factory. At least I thought I was exhausted. Erica was exhausted. She was up at ridiculous hours, breastfeeding him back to sleep while I snored next to her. She thought about bludgeoning me more than once.

Strangers would moon over him when we pushed him around in the stroller. They'd ask us how he was sleeping, if he was sleeping through the night. Erica found their questions to be invasive, like they were judging her as a mother based on how well he was sleeping. She'd smile and play along until the strangers were out of earshot, and then she'd mutter that they should mind their own damn business.

When she wasn't paying attention one day, I hacked into Erica's phone and changed my contact name to "Baby Elliot," along with a particularly goofy photo of him, and in the middle of the night, Erica received a text message from "Baby Elliot" that read: "Come change me, I just shit my pants."

I was a fun parent during that time. Fun Dad. Now I'm so serious all the time. I try to get back to that but don't know how.

When he was grumpy, we'd take off his clothes and let him crawl around in a diaper. When he started walking, we'd take him to the church across the street, where he'd climb the steps with care and diligence, and then run down the wheelchair ramp, with one of us beside him.

At home we'd sit with Elliot on our laps, leafing through a giant board book of barnyard animals.

Elliot pointed. "Cock!"

"That's right! The duck does say 'Quack!'"

"Cock! Cock!"

° ° ° ° ° ° ° °

WITH OUR FAMILY growing, we decided to move out of our apartment, so we started house-hunting. Elliot was a year and a half old at the time. I wasn't thrilled with the house we bought, which is the house I still live in, but Erica loved it. Sure, it was fine, fairly spacious, two storeys, and in a neighbourhood we liked well enough. But there was another house I preferred, and I was determined to win her over.

The one I wanted was an impractical monster of a house. Every floor sloped off into a different direction, depending on the room. If you placed a marble on the floor, it would roll off toward some sinking corner. When I lowered my hand near the floor, I could feel drafts blowing from every direction. The back door was falling off its rotting frame, and a feeble kick or maybe a stiff wind would likely cave the thing right in. To top matters off, this shambling leviathan of a house was priced at the highest point of our budget, higher even, and we'd lose our shirts trying to renovate it back to something habitable. Still, this house was huge, and in the neighbourhood I wanted. I lusted after that big dumb house.

We squabbled over the decision, trying to compromise between her level-headed points and my foolhardy counter-arguments.

"It's solid and it doesn't need any work," she said of the practical house.

"But this one has seventeen hundred square feet," I'd volley back. "My God, we could take up racquetball!"

We were lucky to be buying over the winter, during a slow market season. Houses would sit unsold for weeks at a time, and we had our run of what was available. We could take our time and make a safe decision.

We booked a second viewing of her top-choice house. It was my idea. If we went in with a fresh mindset, she would better see the house's myriad flaws, realize the bedrooms were too small, the basement too dungeon-like. The house lacked closet space and available electrical outlets. Okay, the bathroom was huge, and the main floor had a large open concept that I liked, but no, it wasn't for us. The wear on this 100-year-old house would be obvious to Erica, easily. Anyone with half a mind could see that this was, without any doubt, the wrong house for us.

My plan backfired. The second viewing only reaffirmed her love for this house and its centenarian character, even with me blurting out my criticisms throughout the tour. What's worse, she had been operating under the assumption that I'd requested this second viewing to give it a fair chance, to fall in love with the place and admit that she was right, that this was the right house for us. She didn't think we were there for me to undermine its qualities.

That night I admitted to her that the second viewing had all been a ploy. Of course she was irritated at me. She didn't shout or express her annoyance, but she was disappointed. It was my sneakiness that was the most hurtful part. That's what she told me.

She was right on two accounts. One: Yes, I should not try to fool people. She was my wife and equal and I tried to trick her into hating a house, which is a weird thing to do. And two: I did warm up to her practical house. There was room for us as a family, and the floor was solid all the way through, and not squishy like in the bigger house. We bought it.

We moved in a few days after Christmas. Everyone was on holidays, so it was the perfect time to conscript them into helping us lug boxes. The day we moved happened to be a blizzard. We had parked the U-Haul in the building's loading bay, and we loaded it up as the wild winds whipped and swirled around outside. At the house, we unloaded the truck in two feet of fresh snow.

You don't think, while you're piling boxes into what will be your new dining room, that one day you'll push everything aside to make room for a hospital bed that your wife will waste away in. Some dreams just go astray.

∘ ∘ ∘ ∘ ∘ ∘ ∘ ∘ ∘ ∘

WE HAD DIFFERENT parenting styles.

When Elliot was a baby, she had a specific trick for settling him to sleep. She would lay him against her shoulder while he was in her arms, and she would have a certain bounce-rock-step that settled him down. I would try that same technique, but he would just scream and wail in my arms. God forbid his father try and settle him down. I'd get frustrated and have to put him in his crib.

"Just do what I'm doing," Erica would say, and she'd show me her trick again for the tenth time.

"I try that, but I can't get it the same way," I said. "I think it just reminds him that I'm not you and he gets angrier."

Her technique had a practised precision to it. My attempt to copy her looked like a mean parody of her movements. I would have to try my own thing to get him to sleep.

My need to try out new tactics paid off when Elliot turned a year old and every comforting trick that had once settled him to sleep suddenly stopped working, and only new tactics worked. This was where I shone. I hadn't been weighted down by muscle memory. Erica's techniques were ordered and precise, while mine reeked of improvisation. She was classical music and I was jazz. And, for that brief time, jazz won out.

I have fond memories of those days, being the hero for once, rocking Elliot to sleep, bouncing him on my shoulder while listening to music. Sometimes I'd bounce him double-quick and sometimes I'd rock him slow. I'd find songs that worked well, and we'd listen to them constantly. I still get nostalgic when I hear the Clash, from all the nights we listened to them while I lulled him to bed, maintaining the tempo as I lowered him into his crib, then swaddling his arms inside his blanket before he could twitch himself awake. He was prone to jerking awake from dreams that made his whole body swing wildly.

"What do you think he dreams of to make him react like that?" I asked Erica. "He looks like when a dog has a restless dream."

"Maybe he's fighting ninjas," Erica suggested.

° ° ° ° ° ° ° ° °

WE SPEAK ABOUT our newborn children with reluctance, hesitant to admit the truth. We talk about them like they give us joy, fill a void. We don't say that they drain us. That they deprive us of sleep. Our defences must come down before we can be honest about our kids.

It isn't just that we're worried about how we're perceived. It's not that the truth will make us look like bad parents.

We just don't care to admit that this is how our parents thought about us.

° ° ° ° ° ° ° °

WE WANTED A second child close in age to Elliot. Three years sounded good. Gave us enough time to recover our bearings after the first kid. We'd make use of all those baby clothes that had been boxed up for later.

It was a weird pregnancy. Her baby bump started showing far earlier than it should have. It wasn't a dietary issue — Erica had gotten gestational diabetes during her first pregnancy and knew she had to watch her sugars carefully to avoid that the second time around. She watched what she ate and fought off cravings for sweets whenever she could.

Still, her stomach was getting big, fast. We prepared ourselves for twins.

There was nothing especially ominous about the day things started to turn bad. She left Elliot in my care while she took a bus to a prenatal checkup. I offered her a ride but I think she wanted to prolong her time away from the house and her mothering duties. Elliot and I played with toys and walked to the park. We ate lunch and watched TV. She should have been home by then, so I texted her and asked how things were going. She didn't get back to me for a while, and when she did she said she wasn't able to leave yet, that there was a second ultrasound and some blood work to be done. I asked her if it was twins, and she told me it wasn't twins, and that we would talk later. There was no humour in her response.

Finally, when I was getting around to making dinner, she phoned me.

"What's wrong?" I asked.

"I don't really know," she said. There was a tremor in her voice. "They were doing the ultrasound and they found something."

"With the baby?"

"No, above the womb," she stammered. "They don't know what it is, but it's not something that's supposed to be there."

I took in a deep breath. She didn't need to explain herself further. I knew what she meant.

"Let me come get you," I said. "I can turn off the stove."

"No, there's a bus coming," she said. "I'll see you soon."

∘ ∘ ∘ ∘ ∘ ∘ ∘ ∘ ∘

SOMETIMES I WORRY that all of this came about because of a curse.

When I was nineteen and still living at home, my mom went back to Chile for a few weeks. She had someone else in her life, who was living with us, and he went to Chile too. My brothers had moved out by then and I was on my own.

Obviously, I was going to throw a party. My friends would be there. Some of Erica's friends who were game.

There was catch to this party. Since I was nineteen, I was well into my pretentious, gothic phase. This wasn't going to be some run-of-the-mill cheap-booze/twelve-pack/barf-in-the-sink type of party. This party would be unlike one any of us had ever attended. I took it all very seriously.

I envisioned something like a dinner party. Something extravagant, from a nineteen-year-old's perspective. At that point we mostly just brought drinks to house parties and sat on couches. This would be different. We'd get dressed up well and dine, to start. We'd be dressed up and we'd dine, and we'd consume psychedelic mushrooms. The last part was optional, but I don't think anyone turned the mushrooms down. It was part of the mystique.

The kicker was, I made sure we wouldn't have to pinch our noses at those disgusting mushrooms and chew on the stems and caps like rodents pilfering a garden. No. I ground down all the mushrooms into a fine powder. I hid half the yield in a tray of caramel fudge, and steeped the other half into a rich hot chocolate.

I changed the lights, too, from clear and frosted bulbs to coloured ones, so that each room would emit ethereal glows of reds and blues. At least I had hope for an ethereal glow. The result was harsh and chaotic. That was okay by me, though. I welcomed a vibe like that.

Since we were all nineteen or thereabouts, no one knew how to dress up well beyond what we might wear to a bar. Something with buttons, or sort of clean jeans. And I chose the food I prepared not for its fanciness or quality but because it could cheaply feed the twenty-or-so of us there. I copied a penne with sausage and bell pepper dish from Olive Garden, which was, at the time, my idea of fine dining.

We ate our food and drank our drinks — premixed vodka lemonades were very popular.

We ate the mushrooms and commented on how nobody even tasted them. Was I sure they were even included? We tittered and chatted while waiting for the psychedelics to take effect.

I decided it was time to pull out the Ouija board.

This was the party's real centrepiece.

I wanted us to get dressed, eat dinner, take drugs, and contact a ghost.

A subpar Ouija board would never do. I would never put together an event like this and rely on some rickety plastic fold-out board with "Parker Brothers" scrawled atop it. No, I needed to construct my own Ouija board.

A week before the party, I had found the right piece of plywood for my arts-and-crafts project. I sanded it down smooth and traced letters into it from a stencil I'd purchased. Then I used a penknife to score the letters out so that you would feel the hollow indentations when you ran your finger across it. I had planned red letters sunken into a black board.

Secretly, I had pricked my fingertip and used a little bit of my own blood to prime each of the letters. I was fascinated by witchcraft but had absolutely no working knowledge of it — being a tourist to it, I had no respect for it in practice. You may wonder what I was thinking. I was thinking that this was going to be one hell of a memorable party.

There was a hitch. After I'd painted and glossed the board, the paint was still too sticky, and the planchette — here an upside-down shot glass — wouldn't slide smoothly. It stuttered on the board whenever you tried to move it. How could it reveal the spirit's answers if it couldn't even move? I applied thicker layers of gloss, unaware that this would make the movement worse. Eventually, I had to accept it as it was and carry on.

When the partygoers placed their fingertips on the glass, the planchette continued to be rough and bumpy, exactly as I'd observed earlier. Movement on the board felt forced. Only a few of us were up to summoning a spirit. Most people were mingling and didn't want to join in around the Ouija board yet, so only a few of us were using it. We had our fingertips on the shot glass, feeling it move this way and that. I wasn't convinced people weren't just pushing it, but who's to say?

We all decided to take a walk around the block. The house was hot, some people wanted to smoke. It was a good excuse to bundle up and brave the cold February night. Houses were still decorated in Christmas lights, so we circled the block, gawping at the ever-changing lights whose colours seemed to blur and blend together. I wrapped my arm over Erica's shoulders and kept her warm while we walked. The air was cold, but we were warm from good company and drugs. The walk put us all on the same frequency, and we returned to the house refreshed and in a haze. The mushrooms in our stomachs had branched out to our limbs and our heads. We returned to the Ouija board, under its green and blue lighting.

There were too many of us in the circle, I remember, so that we were squished together at weird angles. We had only room to use one hand each, and when we touched fingertips, we made a circle too large for the planchette, so that none of us was touching the glass. The tips of our fingers made a concentric circle around it.

And when the planchette moved, it *slid*. Like a hockey puck on the ice. Without anyone touching it. Mushrooms be damned, I know what I saw, and I say that glass glided with a force unto itself.

Whoever was controlling the glass identified herself as Mrs. X. We all must have envisioned her in our own ways. I saw an old woman who was very angry with me. She was upset for having been bothered by this snotty group of disrespectful children. When we asked questions, she answered with a sense of annoyance. I felt particularly drawn in by her curmudgeonly mystique, and why not? It was my house, my blood in the board.

The board gave us chaotic answers while people taking notation scribbled away. The answers were vague and fairly off-putting. I wish I could give her answers some dramatic substance here. She didn't threaten anyone, or say anything alarming. We discussed her answers among ourselves as if we were reading a cipher. Eventually, the sense of novelty wore off, and people were leaving the circle.

At no point did we ever close the session. We never said goodbye. I suppose I always expected us to return to the board and recommence the session, but we never did. Mostly, that just indicated how little I actually knew about these sorts of things.

It's not like I could return to the board and bring it to closure later, either. At dawn I took our dog for a walk while the remaining party stragglers slept on couches. When I returned, the board and shot glass were gone.

Simply vanished.

Maybe somebody took them. No one has ever owned up to it. Believe me, I asked everyone.

To this day I'm waiting for the board to return. I'll be in the kitchen preparing dinner, and when I turn around, there it'll be.

My mom still lives at the house, and when I go I don't feel some dark presence like that of an ornery old ghost who's still pissed off about a bit of spiritual fun. I feel neutral. It's a house.

But still. When Erica got sick, I wondered. She was at the party. She'd begged me to take a coloured bulb out of one of the fixtures because her friend drank too much and was having a bad time.

"Sorry," I said to her. "I designed the party so that someone might lose their mind. If it's her, it's her."

That friend never lost her mind that night. No one did. But maybe something attached itself to me that night. Some sort of shadow that's worked its way through me and my family.

Maybe Mrs. X hexed me. I don't know much about hexes.

◦ ◦ ◦ ◦ ◦ ◦ ◦ ◦

I DIDN'T KNOW I was actually afraid of ghosts.

The house Erica and I bought together is over a century old. A lot could have happened within its walls over those hundred years. Who might have lived here in that whole time? Who might have died here? Erica and I both reasoned that someone must have died here in all that time.

For the first few weeks and months of living in the house, I discovered that I was actually terrified of ghosts. Not by daylight, but at night I would turn blind corners and expect to see some apparition in front of me. Every creak and groan of the house's old bones would alert me to some supernatural presence haunting our home.

Who knows what ghosts lived here?

Even though my wife didn't actually die in here, I still see her ghost everywhere. The palimpsest of her time here. She sewed the curtains that still drape our windows. Picture frames on the wall are ones that she picked out.

We kept the reminders of her life and purged the reminders of her death. Like the bathroom cabinets that were cluttered with her meds. Morphine syringes used to keep her last weeks painless.

Her ashes.

Scratch that. I still hadn't gotten rid of her ashes like I'd promised her. That one weighed on my mind.

° ° ° ° ° ° ° °

WE WERE PREPARED for a cancer diagnosis when it came. They had hinted at it from that first ultrasound discovery, the possibility of something malignant growing inside her. They scheduled a meeting for Erica in the Cancer Care building of the hospital. That the meeting was held there was another hint at what was to come. They could have held that meeting in any other wing of the hospital. They could have booked it as an appointment with Erica's prenatal obstetrician, but they chose the cancer ward. Still, you hope that they'll say it was an error, that whatever they saw in the ultrasound was just some anomaly that would pass in no time.

The doctor was matter-of-fact about it. "It's what we thought," he said. "It is cancer.

"Pseudomyxoma peritonei."

"Sudo — sorry?"

The doctor repeated himself. "Pseudomyxoma peritonei. It's cancer of the appendix."

I perked up. This didn't sound so bad. "You can just take the appendix out, can't you?"

"Well, we will," the doctor said. "Buuuut it's not as simple as just removing it. Pseudomyxoma peritonei has certain attributes to it that make this trickier than other cancers. The appendix starts producing little gelatinous orbs that are filled with cancerous cells. And they multiply quickly. This is what's causing your stomach to distend the way it is. We call it jelly belly."

I said, "That's a pretty rude name."

The doctor shrugged. He wasn't the one who named it.

He continued. "When the orbs start moving around the body, they rupture, burst open. That's bad, because the insides are malignant, and they can develop into tumours on whatever organs they touch."

"And the baby?" Erica asked.

"Obviously, we don't want any of that getting on the baby," the doctor said. "But the baby is in its own amniotic sac and that should protect it while it's in there. Uh, do we know if it's a boy or a girl?"

"It's a boy."

"He should be just fine." The doctor let out that practised smile. The gentle bedside-manner smile that told us everything was going to be okay, even if his words alarmed us. "Treatment," he said, guiding the discussion. "The plan is to book a surgery for after the baby is born. We go in and see what we're dealing with. Then we remove all the gelatinous orbs, every single one of them, and make sure they're out, because if there are any left, a single one, it will reproduce into more orbs, and that's the rule, not the exception."

We were back to being alarmed.

"You'll be doing the surgery?" I asked.

"I will."

"Are you good at this sort of, uh, procedure?"

His smile was confident, rehearsed. It said he wasn't a surgeon but a fighter.

"Yes," he said. "You're in great hands."

∘ ∘ ∘ ∘ ∘ ∘ ∘ ∘

ERICA'S GRANDMOTHER MARY also dealt with cancer in her lifetime. She beat it once in the 1990s, but it came back after Elliot was born. She stayed with us long enough to meet Charlie, to witness Erica's own cancer diagnosis. Then she died.

This was not reassuring to us in the least.

While considering Erica's cancer diagnosis over the next few days, Erica and I each independently arrived at a similar theory that Mary had allowed herself to die so that she could guide Erica's recovery from the afterlife. Sacrificed herself to get some sway with the big guy upstairs. It didn't make a lot of sense, but we were eager for any positive development.

"It's like in *Star Wars*," I said, "when Obi-Wan Kenobi lets Darth Vader strike him down, and he vanishes but later has the strength to help out Luke Skywalker as a Force ghost."

Erica nodded without much certainty. "Okay, we can go with that."

Months later, after Erica's death, I was furious with Mary. I felt like she had allowed Erica to die. Like she'd had some say in the matter. That I didn't entirely believe in the afterlife had no bearing on my resentment. She did nothing to help Erica beat cancer from the great beyond. To that end, I did nothing to help Erica beat cancer from here on Earth. Why did I expect a ghost to help her when no one in the corporeal world could do it?

∘ ∘ ∘ ∘ ∘ ∘ ∘ ∘

I STAYED UP late googling symptoms and treatments. It looked grim. Pseudomyxoma peritonei was quite rare, as far as cancers go, and research was scarce. Most sufferers only lasted a few years, and those who did underwent massive surgeries that emptied their bodies of their major organs.

No one famous had suffered of it. That was my barometer.

It wasn't co-signed with a celebrity's name. There was no well-known shorthand for this type of illness. Except for a few scholarly articles, available research for this disease was scant. If Erica had never been diagnosed, I would never have even heard about it.

° ° ° ° ° ° ° °

THE DRASTIC CHANGES happening in Erica's abdomen made her life hellish. The baby and the cancer competed for space, and she bloated painfully. She couldn't stand upright without feeling intense pressure on her back and stomach. Elliot, at two and a half, insisted on climbing her at every opportunity, like a frail human jungle gym. She positioned flanks of pillows so she could sleep, an obscene number that she adjusted and squished into a precise configuration. It didn't help any. Her doctor showed mercy and put her on bedrest, which allowed her to start maternity leave three months early. This was in line with the latest of the doctors' constantly shifting prognoses. They set a date for Charlie to be delivered. Erica was to be induced at the end of July, at month eight of the pregnancy.

This preordained due date would play out in one of two ways. The preferred scenario, according to the doctors, was to chemically induce labour for a vaginal birth. This way, the doctors could give Erica time to recuperate and bond with her newborn before tackling a cancer-removal operation. If labour couldn't be induced for a vaginal birth, then the Plan-B scenario was to cut her open and evict the baby by Caesarean. In that case, oncologists would be on hand to go in and remove the cancer while her insides were available to them. The doctors wanted to avoid this latter scenario to avoid increased complications. Also, giving the oncologists their own space that didn't compete with the obstetricians would result in better work conditions for them. And we were warned that if they opened her up and the cancer turned out to be more than they could handle, they'd have to close her up and reschedule the procedure.

Still, a part of me selfishly rooted for the C-section, if only so we could get a grasp on what was happening inside of her sooner. With Elliot, I didn't take too much interest regarding the baby's gestation. During that pregnancy Erica consulted a baby-tracking app and relayed the information to me — one day the baby was the size of an avocado, and another day the size of a grapefruit. I still didn't particularly care how the baby was developing. I wanted assurance on how her cancer wasn't developing.

The atmosphere for Charlie's delivery was much more aggressive than it was for Elliot's, where we twiddled our thumbs until the kindly nurses graced her with Pitocin, and the lights were dimmed and muted. Here, they wheeled her into an operating room that was palatial in comparison to the dim broom-closet vibe from three years earlier. This place was white and sterile, brightly lit, packed with doctors and nurses and attendees who danced an intricate choreography around my wife. One fed her ice chips from a large plastic cup. Another mucked with her IV, adding fluids or painkillers. I didn't like it. One doctor is a reassuring sight. Too many doctors is cause for panic.

Erica herself remained the central focus throughout, like some bedridden star with a satellite of hospital staff orbiting around her. The nurses had her mostly reclined in a gurney bed, with a drab blanket covering her legs and midsection. The doctors needed to monitor Charlie's heart rate with extra precision, so they used a monitor with individual suction pads that stick directly to the infant's scalp via the birth canal. It looked to me like they'd inserted a pair of earbuds inside Erica, for the baby's listening enjoyment. Maybe some soothing ocean sounds. When they pulled back her blanket to futz with the connection, I could see a set of wires running down her legs to some doohickey placed next to her. I parsed, from their chatter, that the wires were not there to electrocute her genitals like some off-the-books interrogation.

The problem was, the device kept coming disconnected, and they'd lose the baby's heart rate. An alarm would beep, and a nurse would pull back the blanket to reinsert the wires.

"I know I'm getting it in the right spot," the nurse said on the third or fourth attempt. "I can feel the baby's head, and I'm getting there. Maybe he's moving. Somehow it keeps coming off." Knowing what I know today about his non-compliant nature, I can imagine an underbaked Charlie ripping the sticky pads off his own head.

The room became thick with tension every time they lost his heart rate. The doctors were unsure if the dropped signal was a result of a technical glitch or if Charlie was going into cardiac arrest. A doctor said something about transferring Erica to a secondary operating room to begin the C-section. My feelings were mixed.

A nurse decided to give the finicky heart monitor one more chance before they wheeled Erica off. The nurse lifted the blanket up and took a step back in surprise. Lying on the bed between Erica's knees was a motionless newborn. He was purple, and he wasn't moving. Somehow, he had wormed his way out, and Erica, heavily anaesthetized on painkillers, hadn't even noticed. It'd been a few minutes since anyone had last lifted the blanket, and it was anyone's guess how long he'd been lying there.

I couldn't tell if he was breathing. He wasn't crying. He was the unnatural plum colour of a ripened bruise. Erica asked the doctors if everything was okay. I sunk into my chair, sure he was stillborn.

And then the baby curled his thin lips into an O, and he broke the tension with the unmistakable pathetic squeal of a newborn's cry. Those lips flapped when he made the sound. His fingers twisted into a claw-like shape and he lifted his arms for the first time. He looked deranged. He was absolutely beautiful.

Erica sighed with relief. I did not sigh. I cackled.

I couldn't help it. The buildup played hell on my nerves, and I laughed loudly and inappropriately. The staff looked uncomfortable. No one would make eye contact with me.

The part of me that had rooted for the C-section remained disappointed. At least for the time being.

Charlie needed fattening, having been born at an even six pounds, so we supplemented his breast milk with formula. He quickly refused the breast milk altogether. While she'd have never admitted it, I think Erica was grateful for this, because it was a chore to prop him around her dozens of sleep pillows. She couldn't hold him in any way that was comfortable. In a matter of weeks, when she began chemotherapy treatments, she would have to put an end to breastfeeding anyhow.

Her stomach was still distended and protruding. You would have never known it to look at her that she'd already given birth. This wasn't your normal postpartum weight. It looked as if another baby was ready to pop.

BABY CHARLIE WOULD cry and wail. You know, like a baby does. Sometimes our cat, Abbey, would approach to survey the situation. She's mostly a large tuft of white fur with a pair of blue eyeballs. She'd watch as I tried and failed to comfort my crying child. Once or twice she hissed in our direction.

I'd like to think her visits came from a place of concern, that she wanted to ensure my child was being properly cared for. But I really believe her visits betrayed something more threatening. *You'd better shut that thing up*, her expression seemed to convey. *So help me God.*

MY BROTHER PABLO got married a month after Charlie's birth. There are very few good photos of the four of us together, me and Erica and the kids, what with our short time together and with Erica's general refusal to have her photograph taken under her circumstances at the time. But on that day, my favourite family portrait was taken. In it, Erica has Charlie in a rainbow-coloured sling that's wrapped over her shoulders, with Charlie asleep in his little shelter. Only half of his face is visible in the shot. Erica is wearing a black dress, and her hair is tied in a long ponytail that's been tucked to one side. I'm holding Elliot, who's three. He and I are both wearing bowties — mine is purple tartan and real, his is red and has been clipped to his shirt. He's holding a model rocket ship in his hands that he recently picked out, an Apollo-era replica that he refused to put down. Erica's smile is warm and lovely. She was always photogenic. My expression is one of bemused surprise. Elliot is pointing behind the camera into the horizon. We were standing on the grass near the river's edge, and as we tried to focus Elliot toward the camera, a barge passed behind the photographer — the photo captures me saying, "Look, Elliot, a boat!"

There is one other serviceable picture of the four of us, but I don't care much for it. There is a sadness in it. It's from Charlie's first Halloween. He was three months old to the day. The four of us are on the couch. Elliot and I are ready to go trick-or-treating, our jackets already on. In honour of his Apollo spaceship toy, he's dressed in a rocket ship costume that Erica made for him. He's wearing a blue pointed hat and black sweatpants with a fire pattern stitched on. There was no doubt about what his costume was. Kids in his playschool class recognized it as a spaceship. In the photo, Erica is wearing a red dress that was polka dotted with little skulls. Charlie is wearing skeleton pyjamas. I'm dressed in the stripes of an escaped convict. The stripes are faded near the pant cuff from when the Sharpie I used to draw them on ran low on ink. This was the previous year's costume anyhow. I didn't have time this year to make any costumes.

I want to cherish this photo because, like I said, there are so few photos of the four of us. But it's hard to see the joy in it that we're trying so hard to convey. You can see the exhaustion in our faces. Our smiles are just a little too forced. We're tired.

° ° ° ° ° ° ° °

I HAVE NOTICED that so few of my stories about Erica are really about her. They're about me, and she is there. It could be that all stories we tell about others are really about ourselves. Maybe this is a reflection of how I always saw our relationship, that she was a secondary character in my life. I don't think that's the case, but I will concede that maybe I was typically more concerned with my needs than hers.

Part of the problem, too, is that Erica wasn't the type to make herself foolish for the sake of a good story. She was more of a vibe. You felt her presence, and the comforting warmth that came of it. I'm sure she would disagree to an extent.

"I do, too, have stories," I can imagine her saying.

"Oh yeah? Name some."

I asked her sister Jenny for some stories about their childhood, something to really flesh out her personality from back before I met her.

Jenny said, "There was the time we were kids and I fell out of the tree and landed on her. She was judging a tree-climbing contest between me and a neighbour, and while she was under us, a branch broke beneath me and I landed on her."

"But that story isn't about her," I said. "It's about you."

Jenny scrunched her nose, which is something of a familial trait. Erica used to do that too. "Yeah, I guess so."

"So you understand my problem," I said. "How do I translate that feeling you got when you were with her?"

Well, the feeling was this: I wanted to take care of her, even before she got sick, because she had a way of putting everyone else before herself. Her cheeks turned red when I said something to embarrass her. She was keenly attuned to my moods, and she'd suggest I go out and get drunk when she knew I needed to let loose. She loved gossip but never talked badly about her friends unless they really had it coming. She was a generous laugher, but never insincere. And if she was insincere, I was bad at picking it out. She fretted constantly over little things, so I would always try to set her mind at ease.

° ° ° ° ° ° ° °

RAISING A SECOND child was far and away more difficult than just raising the one. This sounds obvious, but I think we took for granted that some things wouldn't get any tougher. We had the parenting techniques, the know-how, the mindset. We had the clothes and the bottles and a stroller.

But her condition. Boy, it hampered things.

Everything became exponentially harder. Meeting both children's needs. Meeting our own. Everything felt like work all the time. Charlie would sleep between us, or in the crib next to our bed, and invariably Elliot would leave his bed in the middle of the night and further push me out. I'd often wake up groggy in Elliot's bed, having switched places when I'd run out of room. We'd spend the day groggy and irritable, me from exhaustion, Erica from the cancer brewing inside her. Mostly, she took to bedrest, glumly, not wanting to entrust all the house duties to me. And for good reason. I did a bad job keeping the house. Grandparents would take loads of dirty laundry from us and return them cleaned and folded. Instead of putting them away, I'd pile the clean clothes up on a chair or in the corner of a room. We didn't own a dishwasher, and the kitchen was constantly chaotic — dirty dishes cluttering the sink, clean dishes in a drying rack, cluttering the counter. The floor was a mess of toys and dirty socks. Parenting didn't feel as fun as it had when there was one kid and we were figuring it out. It had become a chore. We just wanted to appreciate the joys of life with this new baby, but we were too preoccupied with our fear of death.

BEFORE HER SURGERY, Erica was put through an extensive pre-op screening process. She gave blood and urine and answered medical questionnaires. They cleared her for the very high dose of anaesthetic the doctors wanted to use.

She had to be admitted into the hospital the night before, so we took the kids to her parents' and everyone saw her off.

The next morning she was wheeled off to surgery. Charlie was barely two weeks old.

I paced the hospital waiting room, went for walks, stared into books without reading them. All day, people sent me texts wishing Erica good luck.

She spent about nine hours in surgery, the doctors clearing out cancerous blobs from inside her. "Irrigating her," they called it. The surgeon, the one who'd bragged to me earlier, told me, "When we opened her up, it was just *everywhere*."

No wonder her belly had become so distended.

"Then we gave her some chemo, kind of cleaned up everywhere we could, and stitched her back up."

Easy-peasy.

I said, "You mentioned before that every single cell of it has to be cleaned away or it'll come back."

"That's right."

"So?"

The surgeon assessed it and nodded his head. "Don't forget that this surgery was mostly exploratory, to see how bad it was in there." He cleared his throat. "I think we did a good job."

° ° ° ° ° ° ° °

THE ORBS IN Erica's abdomen, the ones that the doctor cleared out. I want you to think about them like mould spores. Little bubbles filled with rot. This is what her appendix had been producing at an alarming rate.

And as her body produced more of these rot bubbles, her belly expanded.

Consider this: Even after Charlie was born, you would have looked at her and thought she was carrying twins.

That's how many cancerous bubbles were inside her.

And sometimes they'd burst.

They'd burst against her bladder, and burst against her kidneys, and burst against her intestines, each time leaving a little splotch of rot. A little stain that would develop into a great big problem soon enough.

And remember, the rot would produce more offending bubbles.

So, even when the appendix was removed, the appendix that started this whole mess, as well as those pesky malignant orbs, we still had to do something about the rot.

And the best thing we had right then to deal with that rot was chemotherapy.

Which absolutely worked.

Some of the time.

Her body and the medicine just needed to co-operate with one another.

◦ ◦ ◦ ◦ ◦ ◦ ◦ ◦ ◦

WE HAD OPTIONS if the chemotherapy was successful. That is, if it was battling the cancer. The first was a more passive approach: Let the treatment do its work. The second was far more aggressive, and something we might want to avoid. If the medicine was working, they would fly us to Calgary and perform an invasive and still fairly experimental procedure called the Sugarbaker method. She would be opened up again, and any cancer cell visible to the eye would be scooped and scraped out of her. I tend to visualize this like a butter knife working the last morsels of peanut butter from the jar, but maybe my brain is compensating because guts make me queasy.

The next step would then be to soak her insides in a chemotherapy bath. The way you might need to soak a dirty pan that was caked in food.

With what research I could find, I learned that many patients of this procedure lost vital organs that had rotted out from the cancer. Intestines had to be severed and reattached like electricians soldering a faulty wire. Huge folds of excess skin and flesh would be stuffed back, stapled into place. Likely, she'd be shitting in a bag for the rest of her life.

This was a best-case scenario.

Still beats dying.

Doctors demanded blood work from week to week, checking numbers and comparing enzymes to see if things were moving in the right direction. They kept the details sparse for us. Whether it was to prevent us from playing armchair doctor or to keep their science shrouded in mystery, I don't know. Maybe they told us exactly what they were doing at every step in great detail, and it just floated on out of my head.

In any case, to have a point of comparison, they needed to establish a baseline.

If the chemotherapy was, in fact, killing the cancerous cells, we could try our hand at this Sugarbaker dealie that I'd really learned so little about.

But if the magic numbers in her blood work regressed, if the chemo had no effect on her cancer, then it meant that their strongest medicine could do nothing for her, and she would be taken off treatment.

It meant a death sentence.

Erica went to that appointment alone, the one that was telling us if the chemotherapy was effective. I don't know what accounts for my absence at such an important appointment. What the doctor planned to tell her would change everything, for better or for worse, and I'm ashamed in retrospect of missing out on that one. I'm tempted to say it was plain selfish cowardice, though that can't be the entire story. I was delivering the kids to their grandparents, and then I stopped at my mom's house to work. Our funds had been in steady decline due to my inability to work through this ordeal. I found focusing on a task to be near impossible. My body hummed all day with anxious energy.

Erica called me.

"So?" I asked.

Erica took a breath.

She said, "It's working."

I felt my whole body go limp. All the tension fizzled out from me. Absolutely drained, I could have slept on the floor in that moment.

"Holy fuck," I said. The energy dip swung back. I immediately perked up and began drumming my fingers on the table.

I told my mom the good news. I finished my work in a daze.

The next few days were euphoric. Absolute bliss. All our pain and anger could be compartmentalized. Things were getting better.

But as the days and weeks crept forward, her stomach continued to expand, despite her not eating.

We took our concerns to her oncologist.

"It stands to reason there'd be some growth," he reasoned. "The treatment has simply reduced the rate of growth, but until we can get all the cancer out, there will still be some growth."

"Look at her stomach," I said. She looked like she was due to birth triplets. "You can't tell me this is normal."

He examined the numbers. Those magic numbers on her blood work. The numbers that showed improvement from the baseline taken in August.

Erica interrupted. "Did you say August?"

"Yes."

"August was before my surgery. My stomach was out to here with cancer. It got emptied out of me and then I started chemo in September. Shouldn't you be comparing this to my blood work in September after I got my surgery?"

"Yes," he said slowly, sorting the timeline in his head.

The oncologist pulled another printout from his folder, for the blood work taken after her surgery.

What happened was this: When comparing blood work over these different times we saw different results. Her blood work in August was pre-surgery, when her guts were filled with cancer. Compared to those circumstances, it looked like her numbers were improving. Anything would have looked like an improvement.

But compared to the blood work taken post-surgery, when the jellied cells had been scooped out and her cancer levels were relatively low, you would see the opposite results. The cancer was still growing inside her, and quickly, even on chemotherapy.

The cancer was growing faster than the chemotherapy could kill it.

Her treatments would have to be stopped.

The doctor returned the sheets of paper to his folder.

"I don't know how that happened," he said by way of apology.

∘ ∘ ∘ ∘ ∘ ∘ ∘ ∘

IF MY TIMELINE is wrong, it's because my memories are unclear. The order is muddled. Things may not have happened the way I think they did.

Erica was always the better mental historian. If she was here, she'd make sure I told it right.

∘ ∘ ∘ ∘ ∘ ∘ ∘ ∘

ERICA COULD NO longer hold down food. She was constipated, and she would throw up anything she ate.

She would be mortified by my putting that in print.

It was a Saturday afternoon. Valentine's Day. The bright afternoon sun threatened to set early in the day. The inside of the house had started to become ragged with mess, since I was trying to handle the cleaning and laundry duties. Charlie was half a year old, and Elliot three years older than that. Their needs were taking the bulk of our focus. Erica had been complaining about her stomach for days. We had a family member watch the kids so that I could take her to the hospital.

We had expected her to come back home in a matter of hours, but she stayed there for the better part of a month. After a day or two, the doctors realized, *whoops*, to top off the indignities, her fucking bowels weren't working anymore. The rot had created a blockage so severe that she could no longer hold down solid food. She loved food. Food was one of her great joys. She kept telling me that when she was finally able to eat again, she'd treat herself to a smoked meat sandwich from a deli we liked. A smoked meat sandwich and an orange soda that she never got to eat.

She talked about the possibility of the doctors operating on her again so that a stent could be placed in her bowels, allowing her to eat. She talked about this invasive treatment with hope, because it would bring her back to a place of normalcy. For whatever reason the procedure never happened. I think they said the stent would also continue to be blocked off by everything growing inside her. Maybe they saw it as a lost cause.

We'd bring the kids to visit her. Me, or her parents. Stressful visits, where we forced smiles and jokes but we were all miserable and sweaty and nervous, and we were all watching our girl die in front of us.

At the beginning of her stay in the hospital, the doctors continued that chipper talk of getting her fixed up so her life could go back to what it was, but every day the tone became grimmer and grimmer.

And one day they told us that it simply wouldn't get better. That the doctors had done what they could, and now it was a waiting game.

The doctor had brought a nurse with him to stand watch while he delivered the news. I don't know for what reason. Maybe as an extra set of hands to restrain me if I flew into a rage. I wanted to rage. I made angry fists under my seat and moaned and stomped the ground. Erica mostly turned her head away, as if she was more embarrassed than angry.

That was just how her face looked to me, though. Because she was angry. Lord, she was certainly angry.

∘∘∘∘∘∘∘∘∘∘

A HOSPITAL IS no place to be when you're dying. Sure, it's filled with nurses and doctors and painkillers. But time is short, and hospitals are boring.

There she lay in her cot. The soft cotton bed sheets and rough linen blankets. Me in an uncomfortable chair across the room, the armrests jammed into my ribs. Like trying to sleep in an airport. Her doctor, along with a half-dozen attendants who'd come waltzing in to gawp at my wife and her incurable condition. They'd ask all manner of questions related to her health and medical history. They didn't know what caused this rare type of cancer. If they could solve it, maybe they could find themselves in a medical journal. Maybe theirs would become the name of some obscure medical procedure.

◦ ◦ ◦ ◦ ◦ ◦ ◦ ◦

IN SOME WAYS, the doctors had always been telling us that Erica's condition was dire. They just used softer language and euphemisms so as to code their main point: that Erica was never going to pull through. Maybe they were trying to instill hope. They say hope is the best healer. But these are the types of people who insist that laughter is the best medicine, so I don't know if their opinion can be trusted.

The doctors' coded language worked insofar as it lightened the despair we felt at the time. Things crumbled around us at a gradual pace and not all at once, so I suppose it could have been worse.

When I replay those conversations we had with doctors and nurses, the conversations that once set my mind at rest, I can pick up on clues, spoken between the lines. There was nothing they could do.

◦ ◦ ◦ ◦ ◦ ◦ ◦ ◦

AT LAST SHE could leave the hospital. We had to persuade the doctors to let her go so she could live some semblance of normal life with her family while she had the time for it. They discharged her from the hospital, but with some major concessions. She would stay rigged to a catheter, because she couldn't expel waste, and she had to protect the PICC line hanging from her chest like a USB dongle. Her father, Ron, and I guided her wheelchair to my car and we drove her home. We were glad to be out of the hospital, after her weeks-long stay, but the drive home lacked any sense of homecoming. We were returning to a place that felt like a ghastly parody of our home. Everything was the same but we were different. It was uncanny. Ron and I supported her from the car to the house, and even still she slipped and fell on the ice. She sat on the icy ground and sobbed at how wretched things had become for her. The kids were watching from the window, and for a while that became one of Elliot's core memories about his mother, that she fell. He'd bring it up to me a lot. Not in a sad way. The rest of us felt horrified for what she was going through, but I suppose he combined her fall with her homecoming, because it came up often. We'd hear it in his babbles when few other words we intelligible.

"Something something Mummy home?"

"That's right, bud, Mommy's home."

"Something something Mummy fell down."

"Yeah, dude. Mommy fell down."

I had been given instructions on how to flush the PICC line clean. I was to give her morphine if her pain became unbearable.

She couldn't eat solid foods but only drink meal supplements, and so she began losing weight in her face and shoulders. But because of the cancer filling her abdomen, her stomach continued to expand.

You would have called her apple-cheeked before they sank and became sallow. Her skin took on an acidic, citrusy smell from the vitamin drinks she had to live on. She considered eating that smoked meat deli sandwich anyway, with the intention of vomiting it back up after. I'd have supported her decision to do it, if that's what she really wanted.

∘ ∘ ∘ ∘ ∘ ∘ ∘ ∘ ∘

THE LIVING ARRANGEMENTS toward the end of her life went like this: She left the house and spent some weeks in a hospital bed. Then she came home and lived upstairs in our bedroom for a few more weeks, getting up to go pee when she had the strength to. Once she lost the strength to get up and carry herself to the bathroom, when she was feeling completely like some neglected shut-in, that's when I had a hospital bed set up in our dining room, moving her to the main floor of the house. She didn't stay in that bed for long. It felt like a long time, like months instead of days, but the time was surprisingly short when I map it out. We were getting very near to the end, you see. Finally, we moved her into hospice care. She was there for a day.

I USED TO sleep on one side of the bed and Erica on the other. Even in rest, our routine was a creature comfort. We swapped sides later when she returned from her extended hospital stay so as to shorten the distance to the bathroom. One night she fell as she was lifting herself out of bed. Her legs, which had become skeletal, gave out and she collapsed to the hardwood.

I reacted the only way I could — by making matters much worse. The fall had awakened me suddenly, and I vaulted myself across the bed to where she lay, and in the dark I stomped on her brittle ankle. She yelped in pain, humiliated twice over. I paced around, apologizing, offering to help her out, to get her anything she needed, mewling at her pathetically until well after she'd returned from the bathroom. The next day, the spot where I'd landed had bruised up like an old banana.

Shortly after that, her nurse put her on a catheter so she wouldn't have to get up and risk any more late-night falls to the bathroom.

° ° ° ° ° ° ° °

ERICA WAS CONFINED to a wheelchair during her grandmother's funeral service. That's how she felt: confined. She didn't have the strength to walk or mingle. People approached her to extend their condolences, for both her grandmother and her current health condition. To go through this at the same time, losing her grandmother to cancer and having cancer herself. With a young child and a newborn, no less. They'd shake their heads and talk about how God tests us.

Erica couldn't stand this. Their pity. "I hate that way they all look at me," she said.

In the reception room after the service, I walked around and spoke with extended family I hadn't seen in some time. Charlie and Elliot were passed from table to table like condiments, everyone snatching a bit of their youth for themselves. For the moment no one was bothering Erica. I could see her moping in her chair. I didn't want to be around her. I could feel myself pitying her, too, and myself.

I was annoyed at Erica for her insensitivity. What an irritating thing for her to do to us all, this dying.

° ° ° ° ° ° ° °

A WEEK BEFORE Erica died, her sister Jenny got married. The couple had pushed up the date to accommodate Erica and make sure she'd be around to see it happen. A friend of Jenny's had volunteered her home so they could cobble together a quick ceremony and reception. Something casual, and without stairs to climb.

I got Erica bathed to the best of my abilities, and her clothes prepared. She couldn't have a conventional bath because of the catheter, and because of the effort getting in and out of the bath, so I needed to wipe her down with a damp towel. She would look away as if to forget this was her husband attending to the task, and not some anonymous nurse. Erica's other sister, Brittany, came by to get herself dressed and to help ready the kids, but I was in charge of readying Erica for the wedding.

Erica had only eight days left until her body had had enough. At the time, we'd never have guessed that time was so scarce. Everyone underestimated just how badly off she was. But she knew. An hour before we planned to leave, Erica told me she wouldn't go to the wedding.

"What are you talking about? Of course you'll come," I said. It was absurd to me that she'd miss out on her sister's wedding.

"I just can't go," she said.

"You don't have to do anything. Everyone will be super accommodating."

"No, I just *can't go.*" Erica wasn't the type to skip out on major events, and neither was she the type to put her needs before others. She would deal with all manner of discomforts just to accommodate the people around her.

I couldn't accept this, because I felt like she needed to be there to see her sister get married. I took it upon myself to root out the source of her insecurities with foolhardy determination. "Are you feeling unwell? Are you worried you'll bring down the vibe?"

"I just can't go," she pleaded.

I'm not proud of it, but I tried guilting her into attending. "You'll regret it if you don't come," I said to her.

"Don't do that," she told me.

"Then come."

"No. I can't."

"Do you need me to stay with you?"

"No. Go."

With no more to discuss, I finished dressing and then emptied her catheter bag and headed to the wedding without her.

Teleconferencing technology was available, thankfully, so we were able to stream the ceremony off one of our phones right to Erica.

As if she was really there with us.

The wedding was bittersweet, as you might imagine. It was homey and intimate, and unlike any wedding I'd ever attended. We laughed and drank and had great conversations, but there was a cloud over it all. I stayed until the kids were played out and ready for bed. I missed Erica and wanted to be with her, but also I wanted to avoid her as I did with all my responsibilities. She was a woman that I loved, and she was dying in my bed.

° ° ° ° ° ° ° ° °

YOU LEARN A lot about people when you watch them enter the house of a dying person. Some people gently knock, quietly enter, so as to not disturb the person or the room itself. Others stomp around and make their presence known right away.

I was okay with people coming into the house loudly, as long as they helped wash some dishes or fold laundry. If a person couldn't help out with some basic chores for me, they could at least have the decency to stay quiet.

∘ ∘ ∘ ∘ ∘ ∘ ∘ ∘

TIME WAS RUNNING short. We needed to preserve every moment.

No pressure. Just savour everything. Easy as that.

Every discussion had weight to it. Its own atmosphere. We tried to reminisce or even create new memories, but mostly we sat or lay quietly with each other. She kept quiet a lot toward the end, lost somewhere in her own head. I can't imagine what storms were brewing in there. It didn't help that we kept her on a steady supply of morphine to relieve her of the constant pain. That kept her head in a fog as well.

These weren't good times.

As much as I wanted to hold on to her, I wanted it to be over.

She was limited in strength, so we watched TV shows together. Shows I couldn't return to after her death.

An uncle of hers suggested a holistic Earth healer who used stones and breath work to expel the illness or some other such horseshit. Services like his appealed to me in the early stages of Erica's treatment when we were looking for comprehensive, natural approaches to supplement her healing. By the time this healer visited, chemo had been a bust, and this man was making a fool of himself.

They took over the second floor with his rituals. I paced the main floor, puttered anxiously while this man sung vibrations at my dying wife. It was obscene.

The cat and I looked at one another, uncomfortable, simply waiting for this person to leave.

∘ ∘ ∘ ∘ ∘ ∘ ∘ ∘ ∘

WE USED SOCIAL media to catch everyone up on Erica's condition. People close to us knew she had cancer, and maybe a few people knew that it wasn't going well. We felt it best to update everyone on her situation in one single Facebook post. A grief counsellor at the hospital guided us on our direction, giving advice not just on what we should tell people, but what we should ask of them, and where we should draw boundaries. "People really just want to help," she told us. "Be specific in the ways that people can help you."

So, I drafted something up and ran it by Erica. We told everyone that she had been diagnosed with cancer, and the medical options available to us hadn't had any positive effects. We acknowledged that people might want to chime in with suggestions for alternative practices, homeopathic treatments, crazy new procedures they'd read in some obscure online article, and, look, while we valued their input and their desire to help, respectfully, could they please not come to us with it. This post was about Erica and not the people reading it. Just because we were letting people in on our personal life, it didn't give them the right to bother us.

In asking for help, I asked people to not send any baking: no cookies or cakes or sugary dainties. Nothing that would leave us feeling both doughy and empty. If they wanted to help, we would accept fruit and frozen dinners. Things of nutritional value. Things from which we could take strength.

People really did want to help. The grief counsellor hadn't been lying. They dropped off groceries and home-preserved applesauce. A work colleague in Montreal ordered us a box of quality food pouches for baby Charlie to stuff his face on. Some folks got us a running credit at a nearby organic food market, and others sent us gift cards for big-box grocers. Someone I hadn't really known, a friend of Erica's mother, started us a crowd-funding page where people could donate. Friends and their families, even strangers, donated money to us. It meant almost everything to me having the financial burden lifted at that time so I could take months off work if I needed to. I could focus on Erica, and on the kids, and, to a lesser extent, me.

It reminded me that it's okay to ask for help.

∘ ∘ ∘ ∘ ∘ ∘ ∘ ∘ ∘

SHE TOLD ME that I shouldn't be alone forever. I don't know if she really meant this so much as felt it was the right thing to say. We'd both always been mildly possessive of one another. This conversation took place in a hospital, and she was still lucid, but it was late in the stages, and we both knew it was the time for these types of conversations.

"We don't need to discuss this," I said.

"I know you won't forget about me," she said, though maybe she was unsure of that. It may have been wishful thinking.

"I'd have to start dating again," I said.

"I've thought about that," she said.

"And?"

She sighed. "I don't like it."

"Well, what if this thing turns around," I suggested, "and you make a recovery and become stronger than ever. Can I go on dates then?"

"Shut up."

∘ ∘ ∘ ∘ ∘ ∘ ∘ ∘ ∘

SHE HAD BEEN home from the hospital for a few weeks, sleeping in our upstairs bed. When she had had enough isolation, we moved her to a bed in the dining room. At least that way she could be with us during the day, instead of tucked away in a corner of the house. It was a more convenient space for the nurse to take care of her, the one who visited us every other day. I know she saw herself as being in the way, a big obstruction for all of us to navigate, but I think she was partly relieved, too. I doubt she could get much sleep in that bed next to me.

We had to put in a request for a hospital-style bed. Professionals brought it over in a truck, and they carried it in piecemeal. All the cushioned parts had been cleaned and were wrapped in hermetically sealed plastic that the specialists removed for us. They bunched our dining table and chairs into the room's corners to fit this lumbering monstrosity.

Erica's dad and I helped her down the steps to the bed downstairs. She was too weak to walk on her own feet, and we considered trying to carry her down the stairs, but we decided against it. Mostly we didn't want to tug at the tube running down her nose, or yank the IV lines in her hand. The safest option was to let her scooch her butt down the stairs, the way a toddler might, one slow step after another. We took her by the shoulders to help her out.

She kept apologizing to us. "I'm sorry," she'd say. Like she was some inconvenience or something. I'd had my share of harsh feelings toward her and her illness in the past weeks, but this was not one of those moments. "I'm sorry," she kept saying.

When the diagnosis turned grim, and she began to feel like a burden, she'd apologize to me, like she wished she could take it all back. Not the cancer necessarily, but that too, of course. But everything. Like she was sorry we'd ended up together just for life to do this to us. Sorry to make us take care of her. Sorry that she went and made human life, and now she was leaving everyone behind.

We finally got her into the dining room and into the bed. I didn't feel very good about her moving there. She must not have either. She'd get very quiet and not talk for long stretches. You hear stories of people who maintain their cheeriness and good humour while on their deathbeds. Not Erica. She was sad and scared and angry. She stewed. Who could blame her?

○ ○ ○ ○ ○ ○ ○ ○

YOU MIGHT WONDER what Erica did all day in her last months, bedridden with nothing to do but feel the clock run out.

It's the same as what I mostly do, even though I'm not bedridden and I can still eat food and walk around without supervision.

Mostly, Erica looked at her phone.

○ ○ ○ ○ ○ ○ ○ ○

WHEN THE NURSE wasn't around, it was my job to administer Erica's morphine at designated times, and when she asked for it. There was no sense holding out on her, or letting her feel pain. She'd stay lucid for short bursts and then become exhausted. With each dosage, or each time I washed her or poured the contents of the catheter bag into the toilet, she felt less like my wife and more like a patient in my home. Certainly, not the girl I fell in love with in high school. We'd been together for all kinds of changes and milestones. They always ended up for the better. So why wouldn't this? Her arms and legs had become thin and frail. Her skin had a sour smell from all the Boost nutritional drinks she drank in lieu of food. I was forever paranoid of her intubation tube being accidentally yanked out from her nose, either by the kids or by me. I had become her caregiver, which was bewildering in addition to being sad. I suppose that, given enough time, most relationships go this route. One partner ends up taking care of the other. You just don't expect to have to look after a baby and his dying mother in the same house at the same time.

o o o o o o o o o

WE MOVED HER into hospice care the day before she died. Just under the wire.

Here's how it went down:

Erica's nurse came by for her scheduled visit. Erica lay in the hospital gurney. Nothing except the dining table had been put away to accommodate the bed, so toys and chairs and blankets and clothing were stacked atop each other like Jenga blocks. The house was chaotic. A surreal, dreamlike feeling enveloped everything. A spectre of death. The house had felt this way for weeks now. I noticed it in my ears, mostly. The world sounded wrong, almost like being underwater. The wrong sounds were clear and the right sounds were muffled.

The kids played in the living room that was adjacent to the dining room, so they could be with their mother but also not. They must have learned a few things about how to disassociate their feelings from their surroundings. Elliot would come to Erica to snuggle against her hand, or to play with the skin at her elbow. He's always been sensory-oriented, and when he'd snuggle someone at that age, he'd pinch the loose skin of their elbows because he liked the way it felt between his fingers. He'd sometimes do this with Erica. Mostly, he left her alone.

The nurse arrived and I, as usual, apologized for the condition of the house. She wouldn't hear of it, and she got to work checking Erica's vitals and her response times. I set to feeding the kids or cleaning the kitchen, probably some unfocused combination where neither got accomplished to satisfaction.

After some time, the nurse called me into a corner of the house where we could talk privately.

"It won't be long now," she told me. Waves of panic and relief came at me simultaneously. I didn't want to lose my wife, but I needed this stage of our lives to be over. Whatever my face gave away, the nurse had seen it hundreds of times. "I know," she said with encouragement. "But now that we're here, I need to ask you what you want."

"Well, I don't want her to die," I said, though I knew that wasn't what she meant.

"Do you want us to move her into hospice care?" she asked.

I looked around the room, at the cluttered corners, the walls clouded with Elliot's fingerprints. Past that, to the paint colours she'd chosen and the curtains she'd sewn. There she was, wasting away in the dining room, in front of our children. She had a living presence in this house that had imprinted itself over everything already. Her dead presence didn't need to be here too.

I said, "I don't want her to die in the house."

"Okay," the nurse said, and she got to making phone calls. There were two hospice centres in the city, and her admission to either of them depended on the number of empty beds available. Sometimes, a bed would become available within hours, sometimes days or weeks. You never knew.

She told me all the beds were currently in use. "Hopefully, one becomes available to her in time," the nurse said.

I couldn't accept this. Once I decided that Erica needed to be moved, it became suddenly imperative that she not die in this house. This became the most important thing to me in a matter of minutes. I paced around nervously, worried I'd have to imagine her corpse here every time I came into the dining room.

But the worry was for nothing. Shortly, the nurse's phone rang and she told me that a bed would be available soon. She would get everything set up for us, including having a stretcher company come and transport her. The nurse told me she had a friend, a pastor, who could come and say a prayer if we wanted that. I said yes for Erica's sake, but the truth is I needed that too.

I called Erica's sister Brittany and asked if she could come take the kids out of the house for us. Bring them to Erica's parents' house for the night. They didn't need to be here to watch her be rolled out of the house forever and for good.

Brittany came and gathered a few days' worth of clothing and toys and books and baby formula. While she was loading the car, I made sure the kids said goodbye to Erica, because I knew it would be the last time they would see each other.

I hoisted Elliot up and nestled him in an open pocket next to Erica and I lifted Erica's arms up and around him.

"Elliot, say goodbye to Mommy."

"Bye, Mommy," Elliot said.

"Tell her you love her."

"I love you, Mommy."

I said, "Erica, you've got to say goodbye to Elliot. Tell him 'I love you.'"

Erica had mostly drifted off into a dream, and her response was muffled, but she managed.

"I love you, Elliot."

I lifted Elliot off her and had him go with Auntie to her car. Then I did the same with Charlie. I lifted him onto her bed and moved Erica's arms to hug him.

"Erica, now I have Charlie here. Tell him you love him."

Her lips barely moved. "I love you, Charlie."

"Good. Thank you. You can sleep now."

I carried Charlie out to the car and, with wet cheeks, gave them all hugs again.

A short time later, the pastor came by to offer a prayer for Erica. He was very respectful, and he didn't seem to mind that neither Erica nor I were especially devout. I held Erica's hand while he talked.

"God, we ask for your kindness in seeing Erica and Gonzalo through this very trying time, and that you give them strength." He spoke more, though I don't remember any of it. My mind was somewhere else, in the car with the children. He asked if there was anything else we should add, anyone to have in our thoughts.

"Our kids," I said. "Erica just had to say goodbye to our kids. They're going to need help getting through this."

He nodded solemnly and asked God to give the kids strength through this. I thought about the boys and cried harder than I had maybe this entire time. None of it felt real and all of it felt too real.

By the time he'd finished his prayer, the stretcher service was arriving to transport Erica to the health facility that would be her last stay. I expected them to take the hospital bed with them, but that was for me to sort out. They lifted her onto their own company gurney and wheeled her out of the house and into their truck. It was shaped like an ambulance but was covered in decals like a moving truck.

Just like that, the house was empty. Quiet. You wouldn't know of the drama and chaos that had filled the house just hours and minutes before.

Except for the mess.

And the hospital bed in the middle of the dining room.

∘ ∘ ∘ ∘ ∘ ∘ ∘ ∘ ∘

SHE DIED ON the last day of winter.

She'd only been in hospice care for one night, but it feels so much longer. Some friends and family visited in that time to say goodbye to someone they'd known their whole lives. They didn't treat it as a last goodbye. No one wanted to admit that this was the end. There'd be more goodbyes to come. They were sure of it.

I made plenty of trips to the cafeteria or the family room so that others could have their private moments with her. I hoped that Erica was able to internalize and appreciate all these visits, but it was hard to tell. We'd speak to her and she could only respond in whispers and mumbles. She was so heavily sedated on morphine that everything must have been like a dream to her. It was hard to tell, because her eyes were always kind of open, kind of fluttering, the way a person's might be during REM sleep. Only a short time before, when we could still take care of her, her sleep schedule had been something like a cat's. She'd be awake at staggered times for four or five hours throughout the day, and she'd nap the rest. Now she was asleep all of the time.

I tried playing music for us in the room. For me, at least. Erica tended to dislike a lot of the music I listened to, so I'd play favourites of hers. I brought along a book we'd picked up for her when she was in the hospital but had been too distracted to read. I tried reading aloud to her, but my voice echoed around the room in a way that made me feel alone, even though she was with me, so I stopped.

That first night in hospice was uneventful, and I woke from an uncomfortable sleep feeling sweaty and irritable. I wanted to go home for a bit. We had a heavy punching bag in the basement that I could beat up, take my aggressions out on. I wanted a shower and fresh change of clothes.

A doctor came by to take note of her condition, and when he was done, I stepped out into the hallway with him to ask if he had any idea what kind of time frame we were looking at.

He shrugged. "You can never tell with something like this. Days or weeks."

"I don't want to be gone when it's her time," I said. "Do I have time to go home and shower?"

"Oh, I'd say so," the doctor said. "Go get yourself sorted out, and she'll be here when you get back."

You would think I'd have been more mistrustful of her doctors after all this time, but I took his words at face value.

Jenny arrived with her wife, and I asked them if they could keep Erica company while I took off for an hour or three. They said they could, so I gathered up my things.

I kissed Erica on the forehead and told her I loved her, that I would be back very soon. She moved her lips but no sound came out. It was okay. I knew she'd tried her best.

It was the last time I'd see her alive.

Minutes after I'd gone, it was over. Jenny said Erica started panting for breath, and she rushed out into the hall to get help. By the time the nurses came, Erica had stopped breathing. It was over.

Jenny called me when I was just blocks away from the facility. She told me I needed to come back right away. That Erica was gone.

I sped back, terrified, guilty for having left her when I did. God, I felt so selfish in that moment. If I'd waited ten more minutes, I could have been there with her.

I stormed back into the building, a ball of fury just trying to hold it together. Jenny and her wife were out in the hallway, sitting on the floor against the wall. They started to get up and console me but I ignored them and burst into Erica's room to see her. Two attendants were straightening her bed sheets to make her more dignified and presentable. I didn't know that the facility would leave her in her bed for a few hours so that family could come pay their respects.

It wasn't like dead bodies in movies, where their eyes are either closed or wide open. Her eyelids were slightly open, but her pupils pointed away from each other, with no strength in them, no fixed point to look at. Her mouth, too, was mostly open, but the muscles in her jaw were doing nothing for her.

I wanted to kiss her, or hug her, do some big dramatic gesture. But, if I'm being honest, seeing her there creeped me out. It was a feeling I'd never experienced from her in all our years together. I knew her skin wouldn't feel right against mine. I didn't want to carry that memory with me.

I did shout, though. And wail. I was still holding my sunglasses from my drive home, and I threw them against the wall. Take that, Death. I shouted, "I love you" at Erica, in case her soul was still somewhere nearby where she could hear it.

Although I knew she couldn't.

You could see it in her expression. She was gone. Completely. There was no denying it.

I left the room and joined the others who were slumped down in the hallway. I was sad she was gone and relieved it was over, which was conflicting. Neither emotion felt especially good.

After a few minutes, I got up to call the rest of her family and some of our close friends.

Most of the calls I made outside. In a cruel irony, it was a beautiful day outside. Signs of spring sprouted everywhere. Chunks of ice cracked and splintered in the road, freshly thawed water running down every slope.

I sat outside on a curb and spoke to loved ones on the phone while my jacket lay folded up beside me.

◦ ◦ ◦ ◦ ◦ ◦ ◦ ◦ ◦

CHARLIE AND ELLIOT had gone with friends for the night. Their grandpa brought them earlier that morning. We didn't know how long Erica would be in hospice for, and the plan was to arrange their care day by day. Turns out we didn't need to plan for long.

After speaking on the phone, I drove out to see the boys. Charlie squawked in my arms. He was too young to understand what had happened even if I told him. I couldn't tell Elliot either, because I didn't plan on spending the night with him. I needed space to rage. One night wouldn't matter, or two. I would tell him when I could.

When I did tell Elliot about his mom, it was a conversation that took place over several days, where I had to establish gently but emphatically, first that Mommy wasn't coming home, and that she wouldn't be coming home. That her body didn't work anymore. That her soul, her feelings and her energy, that's still with us. That that lives inside us, and it'll be with us as long as we choose to keep it.

These are things that we discussed for days, in forty-five–second bursts. Three-year-olds don't make it far into existential conversations.

For the time being, the kids were safe and cared for, which was more than they'd get if they were home with me. I hugged the kids as hard as they would let me, and I drove home to sort myself out.

At last I had the chance to punch the punching bag. I unleashed a fury on that bag, trying to tire myself out but being unable to. I needed to hit this thing forever.

My brothers phoned me to see how I was doing. They and some other friends of mine had arranged to take me out and get me drunk. I was grateful for something to do. It was a Saturday night, and we were going to have a wake.

When my brothers came to pick me up, I asked a favour of them. "Take that hospital bed out of here. I can't stand to look at it." After Erica was transported out of the house, I had called about having the bed picked up and, it being Friday, it was too late to arrange anything. They would come and get it Wednesday. Five goddamned days. My brothers packed the bed up and wheeled it onto the porch where I could ignore it.

That night we went out to a pub and drank and laughed and toasted to Erica, and we hugged and sang karaoke and tried to keep the sadness away. Life was short and any one of us could be gone at any time.

I came home alone to our hundred-year-old house. I opened the porch door and was confronted with the imposing form of the hospital bed, folded up and narrowly in my way. It reminded me immediately of what I was coming home to. My mood soured.

We had got her out of that house just in time. But even though Erica didn't die in there, the ghost of her was everywhere.

THE FIRST FEW days had a dreamlike quality. I didn't get angry or altogether emotional, yet. Mostly, I felt numb and exhausted. Emotionally constipated. I'd fake joy for the kids when we went to the park or stayed in and played. Every raindrop or beam of sunlight might have been a message from their mother, and I chose to find comfort in that.

I threw myself into parenting the kids as hard as I could. I took them to parks and pools and playgrounds so steadily that I found myself burned out in a matter of days. I had been staying up late exercising to battle the stress, and working on her funeral, cobbling together photos that I'd found and that people had sent me into a slideshow.

Gosh, we hadn't even held the funeral yet, and I was already exhausted with the whole thing.

° ° ° ° ° ° ° °

ON THE MORNING of the funeral, the kids and I played with toys and listened to Elton John records, because Erica loved Elton John. While I dressed Elliot, I explained to him the point of the funeral. He knew his mom wasn't coming home, that this was a goodbye, but it hadn't fully sunken in. This wasn't like her time in the hospital, where she was gone but still somewhere else. We couldn't visit her anymore. The funeral was a way of finding closure.

Try making a three-year-old understand this. I dare you.

Brittany came to get the kids so I could get dressed and meet everyone at the service. We had booked a church for the funeral, the same church that Erica and I were nearly married in. This time we actually managed to secure the booking. As I approached the church, my hands shook, and I found friends outside who I could bum cigarettes from. It didn't help. Even though the snow was gone, my teeth were chattering as I was ushered into the waiting room with the rest of the family. I begged for a drink from anyone who might have a flask on hand. No one did, so my brothers took me across the street for a shot of whiskey. I only managed one before someone came to fetch us. The service was beginning.

When all the attendees were seated, they led the family down the corridor to the pews, with me leading the way. Elliot walked beside me, holding my hand. I carried Charlie in my other arm. I felt like I would collapse. I hoped someone would be there to catch Charlie if I did.

Everyone who spoke kept it light with the God talk. I think we were all pretty fucking furious with God at that moment. But Erica would have wanted some mention of faith, even if she wasn't particularly devout. Include it for family's sake.

They projected a slideshow presentation that I'd put together in the days leading up. I could have paid to have someone else assemble it, but Erica always had a do-it-yourself attitude when it came to keeping costs low. She would have appreciated me taking a frugal approach. It gave me an opportunity to reconnect with these photos of her that I'd forgotten or never knew existed. We had them play a couple of bittersweet songs she liked. I can't hear either of those songs without thinking of that day. The bright afternoon sun spiked through the stained glass and washed out our view of the slideshow. Good one, God.

° ° ° ° ° ° ° ° °

I DIDN'T WRITE down my eulogy for Erica. Every time I put pen to paper, I'd scribble everything out and crumple the page. I went through days of this. The funeral took place a week after her death, so there was time to second-guess what I'd say.

"When someone dies of an illness like cancer," I said, "they say that person 'lost a battle.' They lost the battle to cancer. And that may be true in some cases. Her grandmother Mary passed away a few months ago. She'd had cancer, on and off, for thirty years. That's a battle. She fought a battle and eventually it took her.

"Not with Erica, though. It wasn't a battle. It wasn't a fair fight. She was ambushed. This thing came at her fast and without mercy. There was no way she could fight, and by the time we knew what was happening, it was too late."

It was important the eulogy not be just about her illness, this relatively short part of her life that ended up informing so much. She as a person needed to be remembered.

"Once," I said, "Erica sat on a butter tart." The crowd chuckled.

"She would be so mad that I said that. She would make a face at me like she couldn't believe I'd blurt that out. This horrified expression that she made all the time. But also her smile. It was genuine. I'd try to make her laugh as much as I could just to see that smile.

"It isn't fair that her kids don't get to see that smile. That Elliot and Charlie are going to grow up not knowing what kind of person she is. Or the things she'd do for them. I'm sad she won't be around to make Halloween costumes for them. This last Halloween, Elliot asked to go as a rocket ship. Not an astronaut, but the actual ship. She made a hat and a costume with flames coming out at the legs. The kids at his preschool knew what he was immediately. 'Elliot's a rocket ship!'"

I told them about an inside joke we shared from years earlier. "Once, when we were living in Montreal, I was playing a video game, and she was knitting and half-watching. And there was one part where I had to push a button in the game to move on, and I couldn't find it. I spent so long exploring every nook and cranny of that space, but nothing. It wasn't supposed to be hidden, and when I went back to the beginning of the room, I finally saw it clear as day. It was right there but I missed it. Erica said, 'It was right in front of you, dummy.'

"Well, I had been pretty frustrated by the game, so I didn't respond. A few minutes later though, she misplaced one of her knitting needles. Couldn't find it anywhere. Tore up the couch looking for it. Turns out it was in an obvious place that she'd overlooked.

"So I said back at her, 'It was right in front of you, dummy.'

"She hadn't remembered that she had said the same thing to me just earlier. She looked at me with genuine hurt. 'Don't call me a dummy!' she said.

"'What?' I thought she was joking.

"'That was so rude,' she said. 'Calling me a dummy.'

"'You don't remember saying that to me a minute ago when I was playing that level?'

"'I did?'

"'You sure did.'

"We both laughed about it for a long time. And that became a private joke that we'd say to each other whenever it was appropriate. 'It's right in front of you, dummy.' You can all use that now.

"Toward the end, Erica would act apologetic to me. She'd say sorry to me. Sorry for what was happening to her. Sorry for leaving me. As if she had any choice in the matter. I told her, and I'm telling you, because I meant it, that if I had the chance to go back and do it all over, knowing what I know, I'd still do it. I would still be with her. Even if I'd have to lose her again, it would be worth it, just to get to be with her."

I looked to the urn that held her ashes. And then to the kids. Darker times were coming.

○ ○ ○ ○ ○ ○ ○ ○

IT'S A CLICHÉ on TV and in movies for people to compliment a funeral service, as if it had feelings and was capable of receiving compliments.

They say, "It was a nice service."

It was just as well no one lobbed that chestnut at me. How would I even respond to a comment like that?

On TV and in movies, people wax poetic on the nature of death. In the face of a senseless death, of inexplicable loss, they might suggest that "God always has a plan."

I am certain no one had the chutzpah to suggest something like that to me, only because I don't recall knocking anyone's teeth in.

° ° ° ° ° ° ° °

SOMETIME AFTER ERICA'S death, when I didn't need to look after the kids, I drove to the pool to swim laps until my muscles ached, to soak in the womblike warmth of the chlorinated water. Just being in the water changes your core temperature, resets your body so you come out feeling like a different person.

I needed to feel like a different person.

On the way in, I ran into someone from high school. We hadn't spoken in years but we kept up on social media and he knew of my situation. He was speaking on the phone when we made eye contact. "I have to go," he told the person on the line. What I saw in his eyes was something I'd come to recognize in other people who spoke to me in the months following. It wasn't a look of kindness in consoling an old friend. It was responsibility. Obligation.

"*Oh, fuck*," the look said, "*I have to say something to him.*"

∘ ∘ ∘ ∘ ∘ ∘ ∘ ∘ ∘

WE SPENT MOST of our summer at different playgrounds. I was adamant the kids should exhaust themselves at every opportunity, and me too, since they always made me run around and join in their games, standing as their safety guards when they'd climb and run — especially Charlie, who was only nine months old and needed support to walk around. One of my favourite playground games was to pop Charlie into a baby swing and sit cross-legged in the dirt, pushing him as he swung over my head. Sometimes, I'd throw exaggerated punches at his feet while he swung past, and he'd squeal and squirm away.

Nearby, another dad supervised his own kids.

"Just the two?" he asked, motioning to Charlie and Elliot.

"Yeah, thankfully," I said.

"You're lucky," he told me. "You only have the two. Our third is just a few months old. I'm not getting any sleep."

"Is that right?"

"I'll tell you this," he said. "Having three is so much harder than having two. I thought it was going to be easy. You're lucky."

Oh, I thought. *So this is what we're doing. We're going to compare struggles. Does this guy have any idea what he's doing here?*

I considered maybe letting the comment slide. Don't participate. Don't fall into a game of one-upmanship.

It's not fair to ruin a person's day just because I'm grieving.

Still.

I found myself wringing my hands. I leaned in, the way a vulture hunches.

"Not exactly lucky," I told him. I licked my lips and launched into my story of grief and trauma.

Poor guy didn't stand a chance.

° ° ° ° ° ° ° ° °

MY DAYS FELT hazy and confusing. I couldn't account for gaps in my memories from just earlier in the day. Maybe I'd been abducted by aliens. Maybe the gaps were from repressing something horrendous.

I guess to some extent they really were.

I concocted scenarios accounting for the missing time. What if I had murdered someone and then blotted out the experience from my conscious mind? Some kind of Norman Bates scenario. It needn't have been some sick serial-killer–type murder. I could have drifted off at the wheel and run over some lonely old man. How did I know I wasn't really a murderer hiding in plain sight, struggling to keep my guilty memories from spilling into my waking life? I lived in constant fear of being captured for a crime I didn't remember committing. Even when I'd set my mind straight, the lingering dread remained. It always remained.

° ° ° ° ° ° ° ° °

ERICA ASKED THAT her ashes be scattered in a few different places. The first was at St. Laurent, a beach her family went to when she was young. She told me her parents would know where she meant. We picked a day in the early summer when the water was still too cold to comfortably swim in. The kids rode out with Erica's parents. I could have squeezed in but I chose to drive alone. I'd poured a fair amount of her remains into a ceramic owl figure that her grandmother had gifted her at some recent Christmas or birthday. Not all of the remains, because she wanted to be scattered in a few places, but a sizable amount. I tried to rest the ceramic owl on the passenger seat for the symbolic gesture, but I imagined braking suddenly at highway speeds, and the ceramic shattering against the dashboard in a plume of dust. Instead, I tucked the figure safely underneath the seat. On the way I played music she liked, comedy albums she'd laughed at.

We all arrived restless. No one was particularly eager to scatter her remains, but it needed doing if we were going to relax and enjoy the afternoon. It was the only way we could move on.

We dug a hole in the sand. I passed around the owl ceramic and we filled in the hole by handfuls.

I asked Elliot if there was anything he wanted to leave for her, a trinket maybe, or a drawing. A gift that she could remember him by. Observe any child for long enough and you'll know that they can find a toy in anything. Elliot had adopted a Pez dispenser as his newest favourite toy. He would fly it around because he thought it was topped with a rocket ship. It wasn't a rocket ship, though, it was the NHL Stanley Cup. His favourite toy that day was a Stanley Cup Pez dispenser.

We placed this favourite toy in the hole atop her ashes, and we filled the hole back up. I washed out the owl ceramic along with the last granules of her remains in the lake water. Not quite ashes. More granulated than that. More like bone meal.

The day turned out beautiful. The sun peaked high and hot. Wind blew sand into our food, but we made a circle and formed a windbreak.

The kids padded along the shore, their footprints disappearing into the rolling tide. A heaviness fell from our chests. We'd been seeing butterflies a lot since her death, and we took it as a sign when butterflies hovered nearby.

° ° ° ° ° ° ° ° °

ELLIOT STILL DIDN'T quite understand that his mom was really gone, no matter how often I tried to explain it to him. By the time she died, she'd been in the hospital long enough that she'd already become an abstract concept. Someone we visited in the hospital. Someone we saw in the building with the strange hallways where we all pretended not to be sad.

While she was in the hospital, Elliot had been in the middle of a years-long train phase. Our house was situated near a set of train tracks, and we could hear the engine whistling from our house. Some days, when Erica was at home and still healthy, we'd chase the sound of the whistling train to the tracks so we could watch it pass by. We'd tell Elliot to wave and he would, and then we'd walk home discussing what an adventure that was, getting to see the train pass by.

I reused this love of trains later when it was time to leave the hospital. There were smokestacks that towered over the hospital parking lot, and we'd stand outside watching the stacks belch white puffs into the frigid night air. It reminded Elliot of the smoke that blows out the tops of trains.

Later, after Erica's death, we'd sometimes pass a building with a smokestack or with a similar architecture to that of the hospital, and Elliot would suggest we stop and visit her. Maybe we could bring her different medicines to make her feel better, and then she could come home. As if it was that easy.

"Um, bud," I'd say to him from the driver's seat. I'd look at him through the rearview mirror, a lump forming in my throat. "Mom died, bud. She's not getting any better, and she can't come home."

Elliot would consider this while I steeled my face into a hardened grimace, trying to stay focused on the road.

I avoided any route with smokestacks for a long while afterward.

∘ ∘ ∘ ∘ ∘ ∘ ∘ ∘

ELLIOT AND I were taking a walk together in the weeks after Erica's death. The snow had fully melted, and a child with a keen eye could discover treasures in the road. This day he found a hair elastic on the ground. It seemed to be in good condition, good enough for a person to wear, Elliot thought.

He told me, "I'll hold on to this, and we'll wash it and give it to Mommy, and she'll be so happy with it."

I was touched by his generous attitude, even if we were talking about a piece of garbage he found in a back lane. It was a kind gesture. And I hated to interrupt his plans with cold, hard truths, but at the time I worried about Elliot dissociating into a fantasy where his mother was still alive and waiting for him in some hospital room.

"Bud, that's very sweet of you," I said. "I bet Mom would have loved that. But you know you can't give this to her, right? She died, and she isn't coming back, right?"

A little sadly, he said, "Yeah, I know."

We walked for a few minutes, and he continued telling me his plans for this discovered prize of a hair elastic. In the same chipper tone, he said he'd clean it and give it to Auntie. And Auntie would love it and be so happy to receive this gift.

I had always heard about how children can adapt to hardships better than adults because their perceptions of reality aren't as rigid as those of adults. But I'd never quite seen it in such real time. I'll admit that it bothered me somehow, even though I wanted him to move on and adjust. I don't know why. Maybe it's because I couldn't let go of my own sadness quite so easily. Maybe I was jealous of his ability to just change the narrative. The things I would change, if I could.

○ ○ ○ ○ ○ ○ ○ ○ ○

EVERY NIGHT I stayed up too late after the kids fell asleep. It was the only time I had where I felt any freedom, and time for myself. I never used my time responsibly. I would watch TV or play video games, or just scroll around on my phone, daring information to penetrate my fogged-out and exhausted brain. Never did I consider the consequences of staying up so late, its effect on my mood the next day. This time was mine alone, and no one would take it from me.

I woke when the kids woke. My head buzzed, and my stomach ached. I was constantly nauseated from the sleep deprivation. I imagined bugs crawling in the corners of my vision. Everything vibrated all the time.

I would feed them and dress them and strap them in the car and take them to Grandma's. It was so I could work, though I'd usually nap. Somehow, I never fell asleep at a stoplight.

I drove dangerously, in a fog, never entirely certain if this was waking life or a dream. I would mutter at myself to stay awake, to focus, remind myself that I was real and the kids in the back seat were real and the cars flanking me were also very much real. I'd say this out loud with the kids in the back seat. I'd tell myself aloud that I was not on the couch, that I was not allowed to drift off.

I'd drop them off at Grandma's and head home. A block later I'd catch the reflection of their empty car seats in the mirror. I would ask myself if I actually dropped them off. Did I? Did I even bring them to Grandma's at all?

Maybe I left them in the backyard. It's possible I left them, helpless and panicked, on the gravel park pad behind the house.

Naturally, I couldn't call their Grandma and confess these concerns. I couldn't alarm her by asking if I had just dropped the kids off two minutes ago. What would she think of me? But I needed to close the loop and find closure, or else I would worry all day.

So when I called Grandma, it would be under some pretext.

I might say, "When I dropped the kids off, did I bring their bags?" or "Did I pack Charlie's baby formula?"

She might say yes or no, but never did she say, "You didn't bring the kids," so at least I knew I hadn't just left them somewhere.

At least they were safe. Safer than they'd have been with me.

o o o o o o o o o

DURING MANIC EPISODES, I would clean the house and fold the laundry. I'd cook homemade tomato sauce and stock the freezer with jars of the stuff. We'd eat food with actual vegetables and complex carbohydrates. I would exercise, and I would make sure the kids did too. I would start projects, rearranging rooms or engaging in deep cleans. But with no clear path to how I would finish them, my enthusiasm would peter out and then trail off. Hints of a depression would slip into my daily life. Books were abandoned after forty pages. Bicycles that I disassembled with the intention of fixing lay around in pieces for weeks and months at a time. I would phase out nutrients from my diet, relying on inexpensive oven pizzas and cans of diet soda. I would munch on chips and eat spoonfuls of peanut butter instead of the fruit that was mouldering in the crisper. One time I told a bowl of apples to go fuck themselves. In the midst of these depressive episodes, I would look in the recycling bin and see what was going into my body. Just empty carbohydrates. No wonder I was so sad and unmotivated.

I would realize that I had to consciously change my behaviour to pull myself out of my funk. I'd return to a world of nutrients, at least for a while, until the pattern repeated itself. It always repeated itself.

∘∘∘∘∘∘∘∘∘

WHEN ERICA, ELLIOT, and I moved into our house, the front yard was overrun with huge hedges that monopolized an already-small space. We hated those hedges.

For a while we maintained them, trimming them in the spring and summer to keep them from creeping out onto the sidewalk. They stole sunlight from the rest of the lawn, leaving bald patches in the grass.

The summer after Erica's death, I decided to do something about those goddamn hedges. Erica's sister Brittany took the boys out for the evening, and I got the axe out of the shed. I'm sure anyone with landscaping knowledge could provide me with solutions more convenient than swinging a blade into the hedges and their roots, but I doubt any of those potential solutions could match the raw catharsis of chopping those fuckers to bits.

It was a wonderful release to all the stresses that had built up over the recent months. I loved doing it for exactly twenty minutes.

I still had three more hours to go.

By then I was fully committed to this agricultural slaughter. Like everything else related to grieving, the only way out was through.

By the end of the night, I was blistered and exhausted, drenched in sweat and ready to collapse. I'd left a part of myself in that desecrated lawn. Partway through it I had regretted committing to such an arduous task, but once it was done, gosh did it ever feel good.

◦ ◦ ◦ ◦ ◦ ◦ ◦ ◦ ◦

FOR MY FIRST year of single parenting, we lived by the whims of my rage-fits. These tantrums were scary. And exhausting. They left me depleted, shamefaced. I worried about forever losing the kids' faith in me.

Sure, there were a few triggers that set me off, but none was so perilous to our safety as Charlie's air-raid scream. He would get upset and shriek at a frequency that entered my ears and wormed its way to my spine. It was a sound capable of causing me headaches almost immediately. Plug my ears all I wanted, there was no attenuating that frequency.

It was the "Elliot has crossed the line scream."

When I was in another room, maybe folding laundry, maybe spacing out for half a goddamn minute, I would hear a cry, and from the pitch, the urgency, the tremolo, I could stitch the scenario together piece by piece, like a forensic investigator.

Some cries didn't bother me as much. There were subtleties in a cry, and from them I could tell if either of the kids was legitimately hurt, and how bad. Sometimes, they weren't hurt but just angry.

And there was that one cry. Elliot would snatch something from his little brother, or push him over, cause some minor injustice, and Charlie would let out that one shriek.

In better moods I joked that his scream would go from Janis Joplin to Tina Turner.

In worse moods, though, I had no sense of humour about it. That scream made me into a human monster.

Often, I'd respond to the sound by hitting or kicking something inanimate, leaving it dented but not destroyed. Then I myself would begin my own screaming hysterics, shouting every colourful word that my children were forbidden from saying. Instead of releasing the anger, this step usually amped things up, and I'd find another inanimate object to pick on, but this one would get smashed into smithereens.

Violence, then screaming, then back to violence.

I always wanted to calm down. Somewhere in my head, I'd tell myself to take a breath and pivot away from this idiotic charade. It helped nothing and only taught my children to give in to their worst impulses. There was no need to keep destroying, to flex my anger and size at my horrified children. But in the moment, carried away by emotion, I was committed to seeing the process through. It was easier to keep being terrible than it was to stop and reflect on my behaviour.

The thing was, there was never a total loss of self-control, even when I was screaming "fuck" in my kids' faces. I never hit them. I never smashed a window, or put my foot through the TV. I made a point never to destroy anything irreplaceable.

But still I'd stalk. And I'd swear. And I'd smash.

Here's an incomplete list of things I've destroyed:

Storage containers. Kids' toys. Clothes (sometimes I'd try tearing fabric apart with my bare hands, Hulk Hogan–style, and sometimes I'd use my teeth). Furniture. Wall décor.

If you've ever visited my house and wondered why the laundry hamper is doubled over and sagging from the strain, well, that's just because I haven't bothered to replace it yet.

Things became extra precarious when we were getting ready to leave for somewhere. The kids would need to be dressed. I'd fill my backpack with sanitized bottles, formula, snacks, fresh water, wipes, fresh diapers, plastic bags for dirty diapers, toys, soothers, plushies, extra clothes.

None of this is unfamiliar to parents.

But let me tell you about prairie winters.

We had to contend with boots, snow pants, parkas, toques, mittens, scarves. I'd be downstairs dressing them. Then upstairs packing. I'd be uncomfortable, sweating from my armpits and between my legs. My shirt and my underwear would be soaked and in need of changing. My mind would be overburdened, my smile a hideous grimace.

And then, in the chaos, and in the kids' boredom, Elliot would snatch something from Charlie, Charlie would shriek his banshee wail, and I would hit the fucking roof.

Afterward, sitting in a mess of splintered debris, my throat absolutely aching from screaming, the kids off hiding in another room, me feeling lightheaded and absolutely empty, I would at last take stock of what a colossal horse's ass I was. Guilt would stab at my stomach throughout the day, long after the kids had forgotten the incident. Of course I'd apologize immediately, or as close to immediately as I could in my tender, volatile state. Hours later I'd still feel a sick churning in my gut, and I'd bring the incident back up with the kids.

"Boys," I would tell them, "the way I acted today was disgusting. It's true, I was very angry, and yes, I needed to vent that anger, but there are healthy ways to do this, and the way I chose to vent my anger was selfish and inexcusable. You deserve better than that, and I hope you will forgive me."

But, like me, the kids have a low tolerance for heartfelt sincerity, and by the time I finished my soliloquy, their focus would be elsewhere, on their toys or their food or whatever. All conscious memory of my tantrum would have flown from their heads, blown away like leaves in the wind. Of course, that did nothing to assuage my pangs of guilt. It's not my fault kids have poor memories.

° ° ° ° ° ° ° °

THERE IS A divot in the hardwood floor that came into existence during one of my tantrums. Raging, I gripped the broom and swung the bristled end into the welcome mat, like a rock star smashing his guitar into the stage, only pathetic. I'd chosen the welcome mat because it was made of thick turf with a wad of rubber underneath. It scratched up my feet like crazy, but I kept it because it could handle winter boots.

The broom broke. Splintered into smithereens. That had been the intention. If it didn't happen on the first swing, it would sure happen by the last swing.

The kids watched in horror.

Somehow, the broom's plastic edge punctured the rug and left a fat notch in the floor. A divot that you could hide a marble in. I see it every time I clean the floor and have to move the rug aside. It fills me with shame.

But also pride, kind of.

It was a cheap broom. Could you imagine the chaos I could have caused with a quality broom? Wow.

∘ ∘ ∘ ∘ ∘ ∘ ∘ ∘

FRIENDS AND OLD acquaintances would see me and give me a big hug. Their hands atop my shoulders, they would look me in my eyes and gauge what kind of person they were talking to. If I was manic, wild. Or desperate.

"How are you doing? How are the kids?"

I'd refuse to answer that first part, and instead just inhale deeply. "Kids are … yeah, I think they're okay." The air I held in my lungs would be part of my answer. The trapped air would contain all the things I'd rather not say. I wanted people to see the struggle it took just to answer a question. My way of telling them the things that words couldn't say, if they only paid attention.

"They have a father who loves them," they would say.

"Sure," I'd say, and then acquiesce when it became clear they wanted more. "Yes. The kids do."

"You're very brave. I'm so proud of you."

I'd wince.

They'd ask, "Are you getting any help? Any time to yourself?"

"Oh," I'd say. "You know. Grandparents are a godsend. I've been able to exercise and get some nights to myself."

I'd trail off, detach myself from this conversation. I'd wonder, "Where do people get the nerve to talk to me?" From their expressions, I knew my own face was expressing things that my words didn't, but I was unsure of what those things were.

"Well," they'd say, "call me if you need anything. Day or night. I love babysitting."

"You love babysitting?"

"It's been a while, but sure. I would love to babysit. How's that?"

I'll call them on that, is what I'd say, but I knew I wouldn't. It's unlike me to ask for help when I need it, even though I knew people wanted to help. My kids shouldn't be their problem.

Besides, I'd reason, it's not like I can return the favour. It's not like I have it in me to watch someone else's kids.

Until my kids have kids, at least. Then I am going to have to pay it all back. God help me, I'm going to owe the universe so many babysitting hours.

I'm lucky to have my parents and Erica's parents who are very involved in my life and the kids'. Ron and Laury, Erica's parents, feel it's important to be there for the kids, and to be there for me. I take full advantage of their generous nature.

Heaven help me, I can't imagine how some people do it, single parenting in isolation of friends and family. No one to come take the kids for a few hours. I love those rascals, but I need my time away from them. Desperately, sometimes.

How else could I possibly go out and meet someone if I was always cooped up in the house, with all its mess and its memories?

° ° ° ° ° ° ° ° °

SOMETIMES I WOULD get terribly angry at Erica for dying.

Not angry at God, or at the circumstances of her death, but angry at her personally.

Like, how dare she go and fucking die when we needed her?

I know it wasn't her fault. She wasn't on board with dying. What was happening to her made her angry too. And scared. And sad.

There's a rational part of my brain that accepts these emotions for what they are: responses to processing grief. For dealing with a situation beyond my control. It knows that my anger with her doesn't change my love for her.

It's something we don't teach our children. That it's okay to be angry at someone who doesn't deserve it. That these feelings, though irrational, are nothing to be scared of, or ashamed of.

We act like the person who died should be pitied. They should be missed. They don't deserve to have negativity placed upon them. Because the dead need to be honoured.

But that isn't the way our brains work.

So I have to tell them.

Sometimes, when we talk about Erica, or about how our living situation has changed since her death, and the mood becomes dour, I make sure to ask them if they ever get mad at her. Do they ever feel betrayed that she left them? They say they don't know, or that they don't think about it.

So I make sure to tell them that those feelings are okay. We all get those feelings. We should all discuss those feelings.

I know when I die, there are some people in my life who are going to feel super angry at me for going.

That's okay. It's how we get through it.

° ° ° ° ° ° ° °

ONCE, I HAD an outburst in front of Elliot that I always think about. I don't even know what set it off. It was in the weeks after Erica's death, when I was struggling to keep calm. Charlie wouldn't settle to sleep. He was in his crib next to my bed, and he wouldn't stop crying. I was exhausted from having gone to bed too late and was begging Charlie to settle down. Elliot came into my room to see what the racket was about. I remember shouting and throwing something. Not at either child, but out into the hall so that it might smash and break. Still, the act of it so shocked Elliot that he curled up on my bed to make himself small.

If I had seen a child make that manoeuvre in a film, I'd have identified that kid as having been abused. It was a classic defensive strategy, and one that evidently worked because I left the room sobbing rather than throw one more thing. That kid was clearly afraid for his safety.

I was afraid for his safety too.

° ° ° ° ° ° ° °

I'VE STARTED TO take comfort in obscurity. The idea that most of us will be forgotten in three generations.

Oh, sure, maybe we'll be lucky enough to live long enough to create a bond with a great-grandchild who will carry memories of who we were. The way we spoke, the energy we brought into a room.

Maybe we can leave something behind for future generations to appreciate. A piece of art, or a song. Heck, there are actors from a hundred years ago whose names are still known.

Some of us might be lucky enough to be remembered for years and years after we're gone.

But even if we've left something behind, something that people can connect with, those people will never actually know us. They'll just know the things we left behind. They'll never know what it's like to have a conversation with us. They'll never actually get to know us on a personal level.

All that stuff will be gone and forgotten.

Eventually.

But there's comfort to be found in that.

I'd rather people remember me fondly after I'm gone. But after a while, they won't remember me at all.

And that's okay. It takes the pressure off.

∘ ∘ ∘ ∘ ∘ ∘ ∘ ∘

ONE NIGHT CHARLIE woke in the middle of the night and refused to settle down. He kicked and thrashed and refused his bottle. I was exhausted from my late nights and in no mood for him. I'd like to say that I tried every calming technique available to me, that I was a steady and unshakable beacon of patience. But I was unravelling. I had been bottling up my grief. And I had an unruly ten-month-old standing at the edge of his crib and shrieking into my goddamn face.

"Charlie, please!" I shouted back at him. "Shut the fuck up! I'm done!"

You don't need to be a child psychologist to know how that turned out. In time I would learn enough about myself to take a deep breath and walk away for a few minutes. I would learn to take my tongue off the roof of my mouth and embrace the knowledge that hardship was temporary, and the moment would pass. We'd reach a point where Charlie could scream himself into exhaustion, and I could take another shot at dealing with him later.

But in this moment, I chose anger. I screamed into my pillow and then tried to rip it into shreds with my teeth. Then, with sore teeth, I sobbed into the pillow and begged Charlie to just stop.

I lifted the corner of the crib and slammed it to the ground, trying to intimidate him to sleep.

Well. Suffice it to say, that made things worse.

I grabbed Charlie at the armpits and began to shake him. In some corner of my mind, I could picture this working, settling him down, even though I knew I was only a few harsh gestures from whipping his head in all directions and snapping the little bones in his neck.

At least it would quiet him down.

I took my hands off him, horrified, and buried my head in my pillow while he continued to berate me from his crib. His idiot father that nearly killed him.

God, I thought, *everyone would be so mad at me.*

It came to me like one of those nightmare visions before sleep. I would shake Charlie, absolutely throttle him, until his body went limp in my hands. He would quite simply be dead.

In the morning, an ambulance would take him away, and I would be taken away too. It's not like the authorities would turn a blind eye because I was having a bad month.

And what about Elliot? He'd only just lost his mother, and then losing his brother and me too?

I buried my head under my pillow while Charlie screamed at me, his chubby red fingers gripping the crib's bars, his lips quivering.

Dissolving an anti-anxiety pill beneath my tongue wouldn't be enough to calm me down. I knew this from experience.

I had to play out the scenario in my head.

Logically.

If I killed Charlie in his crib, I'd have to kill Elliot too. I'd kill Elliot and then kill myself.

Better keep cool, Gonzalo, or we'll all be dead by morning.

I'd smother Elliot with a pillow, I decided. If I killed Charlie, I'd go into Elliot's room, lie down with him, and then hold a pillow against his face until he stopped breathing. Then I'd go into the basement and hang myself. It'd be easy. I'd fixed a pull-up bar between some ceiling joist — I could tie my belt around the bar and kick off in minutes.

I faced one major logistical problem in killing myself this way. The ceiling in the basement was awfully low. I had to stoop to walk around down there. It's not a great spot for a pull-up bar. What if I measured wrong and left too much slack, and my feet touched the ground? After a brush with death like that, I could lose the nerve to kill myself but still be punished for killing my kids. And who needs that trouble?

I'd need to leave a note too, to at least explain myself. It'd be rude to go out like that, without an explanation. Just horror to anyone coming to check on us.

This brought up a new concern. I couldn't just leave us dead and stinking for some loved one to stumble over days later. That hardly seemed fair.

Scrap the note, then. Best to call someone instead. I would shake Charlie to death, check. Smother Elliot with a pillow, check. Set up the suicide station in the basement, with my neck already ensnared. Call up a loved one. Hang myself. Boom. Easy-peasy.

Wait, another problem: The basement was something of a tin can, and I tended to get terrible cell phone reception down there. Calls were known to cut out. What if I couldn't make the outgoing call?

Okay, kill the kids, done. Set up the suicide station but don't stick my head in the belt loop yet. Come upstairs and make a call. Then rush downstairs and kill myself before emergency services can break the door in.

But, oh shit, I should feed the cat first.

There were so many ways to muck this up. It made me sad, the way I'd felt when I'd thought about launching myself off our twenty-first-floor balcony.

But more than sad, I felt overwhelmed. Panicked. It was all too much to deal with. Executing a murder-suicide takes so much more planning than I'd realized. It was easier to just calm this screaming baby, so much less absurd.

I managed to pull myself out of the spiral. I settled Charlie down.

I was calm. How could I be anything but calm? The tension had completely drained from me. I was new.

Sure, I was also terrified, and terribly ashamed of myself, but I was calm.

Until that night, when I closed my eyes to sleep, I was often confronted with some ghastly vision of my children's deaths. The images had plagued me constantly, keeping me from sleep, so I'd always chased them away with an Ativan. While the pill dissolved I would picture a blank white nothingness until exhaustion overtook me and I could sleep.

After that day though, I stopped pushing the images away. I decided it was my brain's way of dealing with my anxieties, letting them seep away after being coiled up so tight for the whole day.

With my eyes closed, I'd see my kids get ripped apart by dogs, decapitated. I saw their fingernails broken off, their eyeballs skewered and drained from their sockets. They drowned in pools and bathtubs. They were kidnapped and murdered by maniacs, or run over by a truck, leaving smears of blood and grease all over the road. So many nights I imagined holding their lifeless bodies in my arms while I shook and sobbed. It was all as vivid as any real memory. Every time I tried to rest, I had to endure the loss of another loved one.

But after that night, I learned to embrace those awful visions. I stopped blocking them out. I leaned in and let them happen. Letting the images in, letting them play out, was the only way to let them go.

And when the visions had played out fully, my tense body could at last relax, and I could finally fall asleep.

After a few weeks of letting those dark fantasies in, they finally stopped coming to me.

° ° ° ° ° ° ° °

WE SETTLED ON a cold-war arrangement, the kids and me.

I did what I could to keep the three of us happy and calm. All our basic needs would be met. Much of Erica's life insurance money was dedicated to this, to having our immediate wants taken care of. We'd go to the park, go swimming, watch TV. We ate smoothies and takeout pizza, collected toys handed out with drive-thru meals.

The moment one of us decided to break the armistice, the nukes would fly. Charlie would shriek, and I would shout.

Never did the smile on my face feel authentic. I'm sure there were moments of real joy that chased off the monotony of sorrow, but nothing comes to mind. All I can remember is the plaster mask where a real smile should be. *Please don't cry*, it said.

Likely, I never drew in a full breath that entire year. Just shallow breaths that only filled me with dread. Unless I was angry. I could breathe when I was angry. It takes strength to lose patience so completely. I smoked cannabis constantly to take off the edge. I was all edges.

∘ ∘ ∘ ∘ ∘ ∘ ∘ ∘

I JOINED HANDFULS of disparate Facebook groups in lieu of seeing actual friends. One group was especially sexual in nature, and someone asked, "What's the saddest thing you've ever done during sex?" They meant "sad" as in pathetic or embarrassing, but I took it literally. I was out to ruin people's days with my sadness.

"Sometimes," I wrote, "I spritz the air with my dead wife's perfume and then masturbate while the mist descends all around me."

The original poster seemed to be looking for something more banal than that. She wrote, "I hadn't quite prepared myself for this calibre of sadness."

I congratulated myself. *Fuck yes*, I thought. *No one can possibly be as sad as me.*

∘ ∘ ∘ ∘ ∘ ∘ ∘ ∘ ∘

IT WAS ERICA'S request that she be cremated. I was on board with that option. Our city is small and I didn't want to pass by her cemetery on the regular. I'm not the kind of person who takes comfort in visiting a person's grave, but I would feel constantly guilty for not visiting.

In addition to the ashes we scattered at the beach at St. Laurent, she requested that some of her ashes be scattered at Rushing River, where we got engaged.

Years and years went by and I didn't honour that one request. Now I felt guilty whenever I went down to my basement.

It isn't a habitable basement. These old houses in my neighbourhood have cold stone basements that look more like murder dungeons than spaces beneath our dining rooms. The bulk of her ashes were still there, inside a bag, which was inside a box, which was inside another bag. They sat on top of a desk next to an overstock of plates and bowls that we didn't use.

I say ashes. Her "remains," I should say. That's what the professionals call it.

You imagine them to be light. Almost weightless. Because you think of them as ashes. As flakes, something to be carried off by a breeze. But the remains, they had heft. The weight of bone and meat that used to be a person I love.

Why didn't I dispose of them, the way she asked?

It's not like it mattered anymore. She was long dead, and her request to be scattered at Rushing River could mean nothing to her. Not anymore, now that years had passed. It was only for me. But it was a long drive, and I could be doing more with my day than driving all the way the heck there and all the way back.

Maybe I knew that, when the ashes were gone, she'd be gone from the house. Keeping her ashes here was a way of keeping her physically here. Trapped. With us.

That didn't make me feel happy. I knew I needed to finally do something about her remains.

∘ ∘ ∘ ∘ ∘ ∘ ∘ ∘

ERICA BREASTFED ELLIOT. Charlie had to be formula-fed, on account of Erica's chemotherapy treatments poisoning her milk.

It took until my second child's birth to realize how needy these punks can be in the nighttime, because Erica took 100 percent of the workload on nighttime feedings.

Even that word: "feedings." It implies something monstrous. Utterly inhuman. Like a werewolf at full moon.

And Charlie did eat like a monster.

Elliot must have been like this, too, but I'd never bothered to pay attention. I was usually sleeping. Sometimes Erica would deliberately make mention of that, that she was up with Elliot while I snored next to her. To think that throughout all of history, women have been up all night feeding their babies while oblivious fathers slept on next to them. No wonder we take mothers for granted. I didn't even have to physically sit up in bed to feed Charlie, the way Erica had to with Elliot. The crib was pushed up all the way next to my bed so I could stay partially asleep while I draped my arm over the crib and pointed a bottle near Charlie's mouth. Sometimes I'd fall asleep and dribble formula onto his face. But at least he was fed. Good for the bear.

Eventually, I had to move Charlie out of the crib, and it wasn't because he grew too tall for it. He'd stand up in the crib and demand food. Sometimes I would respond quickly, but sometimes I'd let myself drift back to sleep. One time I closed my eyes while he was standing in his crib, and when I opened my eyes, I saw he had fallen back asleep with his neck across the crib's top bar. I couldn't tell if he had strangled himself. I panicked and shook him awake. How long had I been asleep while he lay across the bar? A second? Minutes? He woke up and cried for food. I fed him, quietly sobbing while I did. Charlie's personality had developed, and I knew that if he'd risk choking himself this once, then he'd risk it again. The next day I removed that wall of his crib and pressed my bed against it to create something of an enclosure. Sidecar sleeping, I think they call it. Charlie could crawl into my bed and monopolize my sleeping space, but at least he wouldn't strangle himself while asking for a 2:00 a.m. snack.

IT WASN'T JUST the feedings. I always took Erica for granted in some way. I thought, when we were together, that I was the glue holding the household together. It wasn't even close. She did all the cleaning, the paperwork. She planned the activities and bought their clothes. When we first moved in together, she took on the responsibility of paying the rent and utility bills, and I would pay her my even split. It took years before I understood how mentally taxing it is to be responsible for bill payments.

Sure, I usually did the grocery shopping and made dinner, but she cleaned the bathroom, and wiped the walls and baseboards. She organized the bookshelves. Every Christmas she made a checklist for everyone in the family and let me share equal credit, even though all I did was sign the card.

Now that I'm doing it all, and poorly, I take it back. I was never the glue holding the household together. Not even close. She's the one who kept the household running. I'm baffled that anything gets done around here.

∘ ∘ ∘ ∘ ∘ ∘ ∘ ∘ ∘

THE HALLOWEEN AFTER Erica died, I had a mind to dress up in her clothes and go out as My Dead Wife. I ran the idea past a few friends.

Absolutely none of them thought it was funny, and no one encouraged me to see it through.

∘ ∘ ∘ ∘ ∘ ∘ ∘ ∘ ∘

I'D EXPECTED MY trauma over Erica's death to manifest in nightmares that ruined my sleep or nights spent sobbing on the floor. In fits of rage or days of prolonged moping. And those did happen.

But mostly, it manifested as a fog.

I couldn't sit through a movie without fidgeting. At best, the TV occupied some dusty corner of my attention. I couldn't get through any books. I stared aimlessly at the kitchen pantry when it was time to make dinner. What in the hell was I going to make for these kids?

∘ ∘ ∘ ∘ ∘ ∘ ∘ ∘ ∘

IN MY THIRD year of single parenting, I had a second big health scare, after the blood clot.

Erica's parents, Ron and Laury, had been consistently taking the kids overnight on weekends, and I was reclaiming my Saturday nights. I tended to make the most of those nights, because I was sick of my house and needed to get out. Luckily, I never liked drinking at home with the kids, but I loved going out and drinking, which I did whenever I could. Running away from who I had to be those other nights of the week.

On those nights I discovered a reliable source of MDMA. I used to love taking MDMA before there were kids. It had always come to me infrequently back then, so I loved to swallow a capsule with a friend and go wander the city without guilt. This was before fentanyl deaths from party drugs became common. Now, MDMA unsullied by fentanyl was a big-ticket commodity for me.

It came to me crystallized, like a hunk of pink rock salt. I'd break off chunks of it and swallow them dry. There is no food in nature that you could compare the taste of it to. You could only describe the taste as "chemical." I imagine it's like licking the blacktop at a gas station.

My legs became pistons, and I would dance and chatter and walk until sunrise. Even when plans fell through and I was alone, I would take a dose and pace the house and grind my teeth. I'd still feel great when I woke up. Maybe groggy, but refreshed.

Excited for the cleanness of the drug, I bought a $300 chunk meant to last me a whole summer. Hell, a chunk like that could last a person years if they used it sparingly.

Some friends went to a comedy show one Saturday night for someone's birthday party. I ate a fat hunk of MDMA before heading inside, where I ordered food that I left untouched.

As it happens, ecstasy is the wrong drug to consume when watching stand-up comedy. All you want to do is walk around and talk. I swayed in my chair and waited for the show to end so I could walk home under the night sky.

I woke up late the next morning. On the way to pick up the kids, I bought a drive-thru coffee that was meant to taste like vanilla chai but actually tasted like battery acid. This was my first sign that something was wrong. Colourful spots started to appear in front of my eyes, like the disorientation you get from standing up too quickly. Except the spots appeared even when I hadn't moved. They hovered in front of my eyes all day. I googled heart attack symptoms.

While the kids were at daycare the next day, I drove to the emergency room. The doctors discovered I had an arrhythmic heartbeat. It had always been there, just nothing had ever set it off. The entire body pulses in time, thrums to the same electrical currents. When the heart beats, so, too, does the body. But not my heart. It was beating out of sync.

The doctor started me on a medical drip that slowed my heart rate down to just a few beats per minute. He compared the process to restarting your phone when it runs faulty. Luckily, it worked, or they would have knocked me out and used the paddles to shock my heart steady.

For a week, it was a struggle to exercise. I was weak and terrified of raising my heart rate, for fear of collapsing. Of having my kids find my lifeless body.

So I unrolled my yoga mat and started slow, moving along to an online instructional video. I needed to move carefully to get my heart acclimated. A few months before, I had started doing some yoga sessions at night while the kids slept. I enjoyed it but didn't take it very seriously then. Just something new to mess around with. But over the next few nights, I felt a steadiness return to my heart, and suddenly this thing I had dabbled in became a new lifeline. I took to yoga as if my life depended on it.

∘ ∘ ∘ ∘ ∘ ∘ ∘ ∘

AFTER MY PARENTS separated, I didn't see my father again until the next time I went to Chile. Five years had gone by. I was twelve. Since then, the only contact he'd made were birthday cards that usually arrived a few days late. The cards were always bright and colourful, childish even. As if I was still seven years old in his head.

Rodrigo stayed back in Canada this go round, so we were the same trio travelling together — my mom, Pablo, and me. Pablo would have just turned seventeen. At some point during the trip, my mom told us that our father wanted to see us while we were in the country. We picked up on her tone, the way she said "your father." Like the two had no more connection to one another.

She told us that the decision to meet wasn't my father's, it was ours. She made sure we understood this, that we held all the power. Whether or not we wanted to see him was the only thing that mattered to her.

I answered yes with no hesitation. Pablo was more reserved. He shifted uneasily in his seat as if a knot of bile was working its way through him. I hadn't appreciated at the time how angry he must have felt. How betrayed. This man who was meant to be in our lives had left us. Pablo had been at such an impressionable age then that he'd taken to acting out aggressively. It's likely that he was just as eager as

I was to see our father, but he would never give anyone the satisfaction of looking enthusiastic in that moment. He'd never have shown that he was getting his hopes up.

"Yeah," he answered, cautiously. "Okaaaaay."

At some point in the trip, we ended up at an aunt's house. I don't recall having ever met her before. It turned out we were using her house as a neutral space to see our father. My mom refused to be there, and she left before he could arrive, as was the plan. She suggested once or twice that we not set our expectations too high, as he was as apt to not even show up.

But he did show up. I had planned to stay aloof, to show him that I was still angry, that we didn't need him and had never needed him. But my resolve melted when I saw him come into the room. I'm sure I flew into his arms and hugged him and sobbed and told him I missed him. I felt his stubble against my cheek when I hugged him. A piece of my childhood had come back to me.

Pablo managed to remain aloof. I can't remember if they hugged or not.

We sat down on our aunt's couches, and a moment of uncomfortable silence hung over the room. The kind of silence you might expect after a five-year gap that left us foundationally shattered. No big deal.

When our father spoke, he said the kinds of things an absent father might normally say at a moment like this. How much we'd grown. How he remembered us being much younger and smaller. It was an insulting thing to say, under the circumstances. He told us he was sad to have missed so much.

"Why, then?" I asked him. It was the best I could articulate in the moment. I bet it came out small and pathetic, like a kitten's mewl.

My father looked me up and down. In his absence I had developed an eating disorder and weighed more than most adults. He shrugged and gave us every explanation he could think up. Relationship problems. A need for a change. That he thought we'd thrive without him.

"I knew your mother would do a better job for you with me out of the way," he said. The kind of thing that a narcissist might say. Like we should congratulate him on his better judgment.

Pablo moved himself to the threshold of the sliding doors so that he could smoke and stay a part of the conversation. Our father sat outside, too, and smoked with him. They had something to bond over. Pablo couldn't keep his hackles up forever. Anger is exhausting, and he began to let his vulnerabilities show. Soon, we were starting to get along there, in this strange house, under these strange circumstances. There was hope.

We made a plan to keep in touch so as to not wait five more years without speaking to each other.

These were pre-internet days, and things like texting and video conferencing were the stuff of science fiction, so we decided to keep in touch by phone. On the first Tuesday of each month, at 7:00 p.m. our time, I would call him collect so that my mom wouldn't incur the long-distance costs. I triple-checked the information with him, the phone number and the schedule.

I was excited. At last I could form a real relationship with this stranger that I was so connected to. Exactly what my mother had warned me about.

Back in Winnipeg, on the first Tuesday of February, I just about vibrated with excitement over this phone call. It was all I could think about during my time at school.

I tried to explain it to my friends, but how could any of them understand the importance of a phone call like this? Five years in the making. Plus a month. Five years plus one month in the making. What would we talk about? Boy, what wouldn't we talk about?

At the appointed time, I dialed the operator. I told her I wanted to make a collect call and gave her the outgoing number.

What's important to know, if you've never made a collect call, is that the caller can hear the exchange between the operator and the recipient before the connection is patched through. This means I heard the line dialing and ringing, and the sound of my father picking up the receiver. I heard him say hello in Spanish. In English, the operator told my father that there was a collect call from Gonzalo in Winnipeg for Rody Robotham, and asked if he would accept the charges.

I'm sure my father didn't realize I could hear him.

But I could. I could hear everything.

Can you guess what he said?

He said. "Gonzalo? I don't know any Gonzalo." He said it in English.

And he hung up.

Until then, I'd always wondered why my mom kept trying to temper my excitement.

"Just be careful," she would say to me. She had said it to me all day. "Just don't get your hopes up."

I'd thought she was just being a pessimist.

∘ ∘ ∘ ∘ ∘ ∘ ∘ ∘ ∘

AT TIMES, IN the weeks and months after Erica's death, we'd get offers for Elliot to talk to grief psychologists. I had constantly worried about how her death would affect him, what the trauma could do to his development. There were problems in traditional counselling sessions though. Elliot still didn't possess very strong language skills, and he found it difficult to communicate his feelings to anybody, let alone strangers. I suggested he might benefit from play therapy or art therapy, something where he'd be distracted with a task, allowing him to respond without a filter. None of the psychologists available to him specialized in that sort of thing.

Another problem was that no counsellors ever offered ongoing support. Sessions were one-offs. "Would Elliot like to speak with someone this one time?" — that sort of thing. We couldn't gain ground. The experience was very frustrating. The emotional trauma of the past year had left me foggy and emotionless, and when I did show emotion it was often anger or moodiness. It was enough to take care of myself. I wanted someone to be there for my child when I struggled to provide for him. Just how much would this affect him?

° ° ° ° ° ° ° °

PRAIRIE WINTERS ARE brutally cold. Have you ever seen those videos where someone in the Arctic fills a cup with boiling water and then flings the water into the air? The water doesn't even touch the ground. It turns into mist and gets carried away by the wind. Our winters can get this cold. I've done that experiment myself in the backyard of our house.

But they're not just cold, the winters. They are dry.

We feel the dryness in our hands and elbows, but also in our lips and eyes. It becomes painful to cry, or even to blink. When the first snow falls here, we have maybe thirty-six hours of snowman-making weather — with damp snow that binds and clumps together — before the cold sucks up the moisture and turns the sticky, wet snow into powdered ice. It's little more than cold sand.

This is why winter is a bad time to process one's feelings. No sense crying if tears are going to leave your eyes in physical pain. The body is like a dehydrated piece of jerky meat. If you ever feel yourself becoming emotional and about to cry during a prairie winter, for God's sake, drink a glass of water first.

That first winter alone, we'd get out of the house whenever we could, avoiding the chaos and sadness that came from being there. We stayed busy in the present moment, never thinking about the things that waited for us in our futures or were left behind in our pasts. We'd visit indoor play centres, jungle gyms, trampoline parks. The swimming pool was our favourite destination, if only for the humidity there.

The change room was always a stressful place, either arriving to the pool or leaving it. The kids would hide inside empty lockers while I followed them around with a towel or a pair of shoes. I learned to dress them in their swimwear before leaving the house, under their winter clothes, and stuff their clean underwear in my bag or jacket pocket. In Charlie's case, I'd bring along extra swim diapers in case he made a mess. I chose the pools with the shallowest shallow areas that didn't go above Elliot's chin. I couldn't hold him and Charlie at the same time.

We'd leave hungry and exhausted, sweating from the humid change room where their wet bathing suits had stuck to their legs, and their damp feet had kept their socks from rolling on smoothly. I often left those pool trips angrier than I'd arrived. The kids would fall asleep on the car ride home, sometimes nodding off before we'd even left the parking lot. I looked at them with some jealousy, their open mouths drooling onto their chins. My eyes looked like bruises from the lack of sleep. I knew that if they napped the whole way home, they wouldn't go to sleep at bedtime.

"No sleeping, guys!" I'd holler at them. They'd stir as I raised the volume on the stereo. "This isn't the family car, it's a party car!"

We'd continue the drive home from the pool, all of us awake and annoyed.

∘ ∘ ∘ ∘ ∘ ∘ ∘ ∘

I MADE CHANGES around the house in Erica's absence. For the first time in my life, I didn't need to consult or compromise. I painted the walls and bought new furniture. None of it was terribly bold, just better. A new coffee table to replace the rickety one we'd recovered from some back lane. A couch where you couldn't feel the springs press into your butt cheeks.

Had I been much of an interior designer, I could have gone wild re-personalizing every facet of the house. But I knew my limitations. I could move furniture around all day, but Erica had more vision than me when it came to decorating. I tried to do what she would do, afraid of accidentally fostering a disgusting bachelor aesthetic. We wouldn't live in a house adorned with decorative broadswords or singing fish on the walls. Some things stuck around, like the curtains she sewed for the kids' bedroom and much of the art she selected. It was a relief to be taking care of an environment rather than a person. Houses don't need their catheters emptied.

I stayed up late one night building IKEA furniture in a foul mood. The assembly was fun for the first few pieces of furniture, my sleigh bed and the TV stand, but the work grew tedious. My back hurt, and the instructions seemed purposely vague. I kept having to backtrack steps in the assembly because of mistakes I'd made earlier. While assembling a bookcase, I slipped and put my leg through the thin plywood backing, shredding it in two. I spent the rest of the evening sobbing inside the partially assembled Hemnes.

The next day I drove out to IKEA to exchange the demolished piece. Expecting them to give me grief, I queued up a photo of Erica so I could manipulate some poor customer service employee into giving me a replacement piece. There was no way they could refuse me when faced with that.

I think I wanted the excuse to purge my emotions onto some stranger, to tell some poor employee about the cruel hardships I was being made to endure. She wouldn't deny me a replacement piece, would she, or a refund on the piece? I had rehearsed the way I'd bring this up to this employee: my dead wife, and my two boys, and the piece of bookcase that had been stomped into wood shavings.

But she didn't need to hear an explanation. My preparation was all for nothing. I told her the piece was broken, and she was gone before I could take out my phone and grieve in front of her. She returned minutes later with the replacement piece. I drove home a little disappointed to not have had an impromptu free therapy session.

° ° ° ° ° ° ° °

SOMETIMES, IN THE early months of single parenting, it felt like talking to the kids was a wasted effort. Elliot wasn't especially verbal then, and Charlie was still just a baby. Often, when I spoke to them, I felt like I wasn't speaking to anybody at all. The kids weren't learning conversation so much as getting used to my long-winded soliloquies. It felt like everything that came out of my mouth was filler. No purpose. Just sound for the sake of sound.

For a while when I was a university student in my early twenties, I worked overnights at a video store. It was open all night because the videos it rented were of the X-rated kind. The store had been experiencing theft, so employees were expected to count the entire inventory of items at every shift. They needed to know where the discrepancies were. Every vibrator needed to be accounted for. Every pack of condoms. It was demoralizing and time-consuming. I hated it. I didn't agree to work overnights in a porno store so I could do actual labour. It was supposed to be a quiet place where I could finish my school assignments.

But no, they expected everything to be counted every day. I only worked there two shifts per week, and I didn't plan on being there much longer, so I quickly stopped counting the inventory and just started fudging my numbers based on the last shift's count. Still, I had to go through the motions of pretending to count, because there were security cameras overlooking the store, and I knew they were checked by my employer. I would stand in front of the products and space out, or listen to early morning talk radio, and then I would write down the exact number that was marked by the person in the last shift, unless I knew something had been purchased. If I eventually got in trouble for faking my way through work, then so be it. I wouldn't be at this job forever.

I was pretending to work, faking my way through the steps for the benefit of cameras that may or may not have been checked at some later point. That's how I felt later, talking to the kids. I didn't know why I was doing it and I didn't know who it was for.

Under ideal circumstances, the kids would have heard me talking to their mom. Natural conversation between adults, patter that would allow the kids to discover our personalities. Now, I had no one in the house I wanted to speak with. Every time I talked, I felt like that university kid again. Faking it, just for pretend.

° ° ° ° ° ° ° °

WE PLAYED IN the front yard until the skies streaked orange and red. It was summertime, and Charlie had just turned two. The boys took turns pulling one another in the wagon, up and down the sidewalk. The house sits at a slope in the road, and dips down when you take a left.

You always take a left when you leave the house. Who wants to walk uphill?

On this evening Charlie sat in the wagon and Elliot pulled him to the sidewalk's apex. Then Elliot ran back down the slope, pulling the wagon behind him. At the bottom of the slope, my neighbour's chain link fence jutted onto the concrete. Just a bit. Just enough.

Don't get ahead of me.

The wagon hit the fence and Charlie flew forward, like a crash test dummy through the windshield. He flipped over, pivoting on his face the way a vaulter's pole pivots in the earth. Luckily, the pivot was in the grass and not the concrete, so he didn't rip his face to shreds. This doesn't end up with a trip to the emergency room. But he was left with a shiner. You could have dressed him convincingly like an old-time baseball player, or like a raccoon nesting in your attic.

This wouldn't have been so bad if Elliot hadn't also been recovering from a black eye, having socked himself on a toy the week before.

One single dad and two kids with black eyes. It's a bad look, even if you are just doing your best.

◦ ◦ ◦ ◦ ◦ ◦ ◦ ◦ ◦

THE CHURCH WHERE we held Erica's funeral is not far from our house. The other end of our neighbourhood. A twenty minute walk, maybe.

You can sometimes hear the church bells tolling from our house. On a quiet evening, say.

Like a little reminder, sometimes intruding.

That's the worst. When memories feel like intrusions.

When she pops into my head and I think, "Shit, I have to think of her now." As much as I loved her, and still do, some days I don't want to think about her.

Maybe I'll be outside watching a squirrel leap off a telephone pole into a tree. Maybe talking to a neighbour from the block while our kids play on the trampoline. Parents getting to have a grown-up conversation, which is a luxury. And then the church bells will chime and I'll remember her funeral. Whatever I was focusing on, it's gone.

Sometimes it's nice to remember, and sometimes it's a pain in the ass.

◦ ◦ ◦ ◦ ◦ ◦ ◦ ◦ ◦

THIS IS THE first of three camping stories. I'll start with the most recent of the bunch, well after the kids and I had adjusted to our lives as a trio. Charlie would have just turned six, and Elliot nine. We went with family — mom, step-dad, niece, and nephew.

During our last night in the woods, I woke to the sound of rustling in the kitchen tent. Some animal was rooting around our stuff, searching for food. Neither of the kids had woken up. I could hear muffled chattering over at the next tent, where everyone else was sleeping. I tried scaring the creature off by making grunts from inside my tent, giving the scavenger a chance to clear out at the sound of an irritable human. The clamouring continued. I wasn't especially keen on confronting the animal, alone in the dark, but I decided that I needed to pee anyway, so I took out my phone and turned on the flashlight. It was four in the morning.

I unzipped the tent and stepped into the brisk night air, wearing only a pair of boxer briefs. Not like clothes would be of any use against a bear anyhow.

Sure, it might have been a raccoon pawing through our stuff. That was entirely possible. But I had decided that the creature had to be a bear. It could be nothing else.

Here's why I had decided it was a bear: In the campground bathrooms, the parkies had taped up flyers warning people to be Bear Smart. Then hung them in the stalls and over the sinks. The flyers warned people not to leave food out, and showed a picture of a large black bear knocking over trash bins. There was an example of an appropriately tidy campsite that was clear of food, and another inappropriate one that was messy with food.

Well, I had been overtaken with the childish urge to commit vandalism, so earlier in the day I'd brought a pen into the bathroom and made a few edits to the flyer above the sink. Now it warned people to be Beans Smart. The clean campsite proudly bragged, "No Beans!" I drew empty tin cans amid the debris of the messy site and added a frowny face: "Beans!" I gave the bear a large thought bubble that proclaimed its undying love for beans. "Please report any beans sightings to park officers," the flyer now warned. "Bears love beans."

Not content with simply committing vandalism and carrying on quietly, I took a photo of my work and later boasted to the kids about my hijinks. "Look, boys," I said to them. "Beans!" They screwed up their faces at me when I told them my original idea to have made the flyer say, "Be Beard Smart," and give the bear a great big bushy beard. "Please report any beard sightings to park officials," it would have said. I suggested we graffiti another flyer in some other part of the campground.

So while I was stepping into the night, ready to confront some nocturnal creature that was eating our food, armed with only a cell phone flashlight, wearing only a pair of underpants, I thought, *The bears have come to teach me a lesson*. This was poetic justice.

I approached the kitchen tent growling a raw sound from the back of my throat, trying to spook the poor creature out of our site. My parents, who were now watching from the cover of their own tent, hissed at me to be careful.

I waved the flashlight around but could see no animal. It was likely in the trees, waiting for me to leave. I could see the corner of the tent had been disturbed, but not terribly, so I returned the flap over the cooler and then shuffled away to pee in the treeline away from the animal. I kept on with the guttural noises so as to alert any animals to my presence.

Content that that animal had retreated, I returned to the kids in my own tent, replaying the scene in my head. The tent. The cooler.

Oh, jeez, I thought to myself. Nobody had bothered to put the cooler into a vehicle. I certainly didn't think to do that, in my underwear, in the cool night air. I had just left it out for the bear to have at.

The rummaging noises continued. I had left and the animal had returned.

I hollered over to my parents in the next tent. "Hey, guys. I just realized the cooler is still out there."

"It's fine," my mom answered. "Don't go back out there."

"I wasn't planning on it," I said, shaking off the cold. We were both relieved that I hadn't been devoured by anything out there. "I just mean that we might not have any breakfast left tomorrow."

"We'll figure it out," she said.

The rustling sounds grew noisier and more urgent. Whatever was out there had become emboldened in my absence. After a few minutes, I had the sense to fish my cars keys out of my backpack and double-clicked the unlock button, flashing my car's headlights, which seemed at last enough to scare the thing off.

When I woke again in the morning, my mother was already awake and packing up the kitchen tent.

"How's the breakfast situation?" I asked.

She sighed and motioned vaguely to the busted food cooler. "It's all gone," she said. "It ate all the eggs and the sausages and even licked the butter out of the container."

I followed the minor wreckage out into the treeline where the animal had left the evidence of its plunder. I guessed that it had dragged the food into the trees so that it could eat, and likely returned to the site for more. We went over the crime scene like forensic investigators.

It wasn't all that bad. There was a diner in town a short drive away. My mom seemed a little peeved that the bear had absconded with all our food, since she was looking forward to a last breakfast around the picnic table.

But Charlie, who was listening nearby, blurted out something that made us laugh, and that gave us some perspective.

"Well," he said, "good for the bear."

∘ ∘ ∘ ∘ ∘ ∘ ∘ ∘

I DIDN'T SEE my father for years.

Which isn't to say I didn't have a father figure in my life. After my parents split up, but before I tried reconnecting with my father, my mom found someone else to be part of her life. Another Chilean refugee named Julio. He's been a good man to her and to me this whole time. He's been in my life since I was about eight. I'll admit that my walls were up when he came into our lives, and those walls have never fully come down. That's just the way of it. I've never called him Dad, and only recently have I collectively referred to him and my mom as my parents. It'd always been "my mom and her partner."

My biological father still sent me childish birthday cards every other year. Once or twice he wrote about how he missed me and my brothers, and that his heart hurt to not be a part of our lives. I didn't know at the time that he'd started a new family, and I had half-siblings I've still never met.

I guess time was moving forward for everyone, and not just me.

I also grew up. I got married. Had two children. My wife died. I had to stray strong for the kids. At the very least, I had to not fall apart.

My father made contact with me after Erica's death. Someone must have given him my email address, a relative, maybe. He might have reached out to me directly on Facebook. I can't remember. The details are a blur.

He told me that he had suffered a heart attack recently. A second heart attack, actually, and he was looking to set things right, to fix the things in his life. I was just beginning to understand this point myself, that life was short and grudges were pointless. But it still didn't mean I would trust this man with my emotions, that I'd open up and be vulnerable with him again. Was he crazy?

We sent a few messages back and forth and decided to chat through a video conferencing app. Technology had caught up to us, and we were no longer confined to post office mail and collect calls.

We talked while I cooked dinner and the kids played in front of the TV. I wouldn't even give my father my full attention. He needed to earn that. He didn't bring up Erica's death, though I was sure he knew about it. She had only been dead a few weeks and the timing was too coincidental. I was convinced he was using the emotional void in my heart to weasel his way back into my life, just so he could ditch me again. After a while he asked where my wife was.

"What are you talking about?" I said to him. "You know where she is."

"I don't," he said.

I sighed and put down the cooking utensils. The phone was propped up on a shelf at eye level so I could talk in front of the stove.

"You really don't know?" I asked. I was sure I was being coerced into telling him something that didn't need explaining. I thought he was being cruel.

"I don't know," he said.

"She died," I told him. "She got cancer and died. Didn't anyone tell you?"

"Oh, nooo," he said. He groaned, "Ahhhh," like a poor performance of someone grieving. I rolled my eyes.

"Okay," I said. "Yeah, a few weeks ago. So it's just me and the kids."

"Gonzalo," he said, "I wish that I could do something for you. To take the kids so you could rest or have some peace."

"Yeah, well."

I was glad for dinner to be ready so that I could end the call. His whole manner struck me as insincere and off-putting. I told my mom about it later, and while she isn't the type to ever believe my father, she wasn't sure anyone had actually talked to him about Erica's death. Maybe his put-on response was legitimate, if overblown.

I decided over the next month to give my father a chance. A real chance. But I needed to do something first. I needed to clear the table, as it were. I decided I would let my father back into my life.

I just needed to tell him off first.

He would need to hear it all. Every gripe, every feeling of anxiety. I would need to tell him that I heard him refuse my collect call, deny even knowing my name. If we were to form a relationship, we would need to settle all these old problems and insecurities that had bothered me from the day he left.

It was decided. All I needed to do was get around to it.

Because I was reticent to invite him back into my life, I kept putting it off. Life itself in those days was a constant source of stress and sadness, and it didn't feel like the time to introduce more bad feelings into my life. So I waited for it to happen organically. Maybe my father would ask to have another video chat and I could spew out all the things that I had been silently rehearsing all this time.

Then he went and died.

That fucker.

It was a third heart attack that took him out.

To be honest, I wasn't terribly sad that he died. Nor did I regret missing out on fixing our broken relationship. I was already annoyed that this guy had outlived my wife. But it irritated me that all these thoughts and feelings had built up inside me and had nowhere to go. If I regretted missing out on anything, it was missing the opportunity to tell my father to go fuck himself. Just one good "eat shit" before he died. Who knows how I'd feel about him now if we'd allowed ourselves to move past that.

So let this be a lesson. Don't wait until it's too late to tell someone to fuck off.

° ° ° ° ° ° ° °

I HAVE A stack of photos lying around in an envelope. It turns up periodically, and when it does, I leaf through them, consider throwing them out, decide against it, then return them to the envelope and leave them where I found them. They are not well preserved, and eventually the basement's humidity will make them stick together, ruining them.

They're pictures of me and Erica and the boys. Most of them aren't great photos — they're hastily taken and out of focus. One of the better ones is of Elliot posing with baby Charlie in front of their mom. It should be on our wall. But look more closely. See the drab grey of hospital bedsheets. The hint of a hospital food tray inching into the frame. It's during a visit from the kids while Erica was in the hospital. She was dying there and we didn't yet know it.

Elliot once discovered these photos and insisted on putting them out on display. For a few days, I was confronted by these pictures that clouded my mood. So I took them down. But still, I couldn't throw them out, so back into the envelope they went, into the basement. Treasure to be discovered later. Upsetting photos to be unearthed.

Why can't I throw these pictures out? Maybe I know they're a document to something important, a moment in time that isn't always easy but is always the truth. Maybe I hope that time will temper the hurt I feel whenever I see these pictures. It never works. Every time they re-emerge, I'm never any more comfortable with them.

Whenever they turn up again, I can maybe almost hopefully come close to nearly deciding to one day throw them out.

◦ ◦ ◦ ◦ ◦ ◦ ◦ ◦

WE GROW UP and learn to define our traumas. We see therapists and take psychedelics to get to the root of them. It's our duty to ourselves, to our loved ones, to exorcise these traumas or at least learn to live with them so that they can no longer control us.

We all have trauma. At a certain point, it's no excuse for being an asshole.

But, in an attempt to connect a child with a dead parent, we have to instill the trauma in them. Make it a part of their origin story. Make it so they can never forget. They're forced to remember what they've lost when we remind them of what's gone. It's meant with the best of intentions.

"What a great drawing," we say. "You know your mom was a great artist. She'd be so proud of you."

What a kind way to remind children of their traumatic past.

Your mother would have been so proud of you.

° ° ° ° ° ° ° ° °

THE PROBLEM WITH being the lone adult in the house is that there is no one to keep me in check when I make poor executive decisions. Over the years this problem hasn't gone away.

I'm trying to decide if I should spend money on a tattoo or to go see a psychic. Meanwhile, I'm two years behind on my taxes. I owe thousands of dollars in bills and credit card debt. One of my molars hurts when I eat, and it needs to be fixed before it crumbles in my mouth.

Still, a tattoo would be nice. It'd be good for the bear.

° ° ° ° ° ° ° ° °

I TOLD MY friends about the ways lately that Charlie was trying to get my goat. We were butting heads at the time, Charlie and me. I thought he'd grow out of his terrible twos early, but a lot of his poor social habits became amplified over time. Sometimes, he'd try to be overtly obnoxious, but sometimes he would just pick the wrong moments to be goofy. Often, he would just be too tired to be reasoned with, and he'd repeat songs or phrases ad infinitum until I was ready to launch him out the window.

Once, it was the other way around. I was bragging to friends about all the ways in which I'd annoy Charlie. I took a video of him napping on the couch while I tried to wake him up by bouncing an inflated balloon off his face. The balloon would thud off his cheeks and I would laugh about it while he slept on. I relayed the story, still giggling at the memory.

One friend leaned in and told me, "You really have the kids you deserve."

◦ ◦ ◦ ◦ ◦ ◦ ◦ ◦ ◦

ANOTHER STORY ABOUT camping. This was the year after Erica's death. Four full seasons had gone by.

The adults let the kids sleep in their own tent. Elliot was asleep next to Charlie and another child from our group. The adults sat around the fire, and at one moment we looked up to admire the stars. They peppered the sky in glimmers of light. What's more, they had depth. You could gauge relative distances between each one. Stare longer and the details develop. You feel a pull, like tides.

Elliot was five or six years old and in love with the concept of the stars. I say "concept" because he never got to stay up late enough to properly experience them. I wanted to change that. I told the other adults in our camping party that I was going to wake him up and show him this gorgeous starry sky. He would appreciate it. But I knew he wouldn't appreciate being forced out of bed, marched out into the chilly night, and ordered to look at the stars. And he couldn't just pop his head out of the tent to look, because we had put a tarp over the campsite after a recent downpour.

There was a place I could take him to. A clearing just down the gravel road, not a minute's walk away. Two minutes tops. There, the trees parted and a wide sky opened. What if I could scoop him and wrap him in a blanket. I could carry him out of the tent and to the clearing in the road where the trees gave way and Elliot could look at every constellation with only the naked eye. If someone could keep tabs on Charlie while I was gone, I asked, and the adults told me they could keep eyes on him.

I stepped into the kids' tent and tried to pull Elliot up while he was still sleeping. I hoped it would be a smooth transfer, like when I'd wake them from their car seats and carry them inside. I wanted Elliot to not remember the journey out, but just waking up under night sky. I wanted the experience to feel hazy but profound, something he thinks about periodically in his adult life as this strange mental snapshot that could be a memory or could be a fever dream.

Elliot resisted me immediately. "What's happening?" he asked, while I hauled him out.

"It's a surprise," I said. "Stay wrapped up. Stay warm."

He snuggled in but seemed put off by the experience. No matter. I would press on. I picked up the pace. We'd be at the clearing in a minute. Two tops. But as I walked, I started to feel duped by my own memory. What I thought was minutes in the ambling daylight had become much longer. I passed a campsite that had been lit up for a small party. A few of them noticed me carrying a child and greeted me with warmth.

"How's it going?" someone said to me. "Stay careful. There's a skunk out there."

"You don't say," I answered. "I'll pay attention."

Elliot lifted his head off my shoulder. "Skunk?"

I said, "Don't worry about it. Put your head down."

He didn't put his head down. And he absolutely continued to worry about it.

"There's a skunk?"

"So they say, bud."

"An actual skunk?"

"It's okay," I said. "It won't spray us if we don't scare it. We'll make sure not to scare it. Put your head down, bud. You're getting heavy to carry."

"But what if the skunk sprays us?"

"Listen," I said, "when you put your head down, it makes you easier to carry. But for the skunk, don't worry, we're almost where we're going?"

"Where are we going?" he asked.

"It's a surprise. Put your head down."

We eventually did reach the clearing. It really was wonderful to look at. My forearms ached from being locked in place so long. I bounced my legs in place to retain blood circulation.

I told Elliot to lift his head off my shoulder and look. The sky really was impressive.

After a few minutes, he was cold and unnerved, and he wanted to go back to the tent.

The next morning I asked him if he remembered how the sky looked the night before. He didn't. The experience seemed to have been for nothing. All he remembered about the night before was narrowly avoiding a skunk.

○ ○ ○ ○ ○ ○ ○ ○

EVERY TIME I give the house a deep clean, I manage to get rid of more of her things. At first I was reluctant to toss anything. The house needed to remain something of a shrine to our poor dead wife and mother. Who knew how much of this stuff the kids would need to be able to reconstruct who she was as a person? But now, whenever the storage space gets an overhaul, those precious possessions become just that: stuff. It gets donated, parted with. After a while only the most essential of things are kept. Distilled down to her most essential.

Curiously enough, sometimes the kids discover things that Erica must have owned but never particularly cared about. Jewellery that she didn't wear, clothes not in her style. Things of no importance that I'd never given to her sisters or donated. They find these things and act like these trinkets were of some great value to their mom. I have to break it to them.

"Those earrings weren't her style," I'd say. "I've never seen her wear that scarf. I don't know why we have that here."

It distorts their perspectives of her. I guess no matter how I try to shape their memories of her, they'll fill in the gaps however they want to.

There are still a few things I refuse to get rid of. There's a Batman toy somewhere in the basement that neither of them had played with for years. There is nothing obviously special about it — it's just a generic plastic action figure. But it was the last thing Erica had bought for the kids. She ordered it, and then she died, and then it arrived in the mail. I can't get rid of that.

° ° ° ° ° ° ° °

WE HAD NOTICED that something was up with Elliot since he was a toddler. Unusual traits. He'd become upset if there was a sudden change in his surroundings. Someone putting away his toys abruptly, or taking him to bed without warning. Some things are just kids being kids, right? So what if his auntie showing up unexpectedly, grinning at him and saying, "Hi, Boo," would throw him into hysterics? That was just him being a weirdo. Kids are weirdos.

But there were other clues. He was late to the game in speaking, for one.

His two-year checkup put a sense of urgency around it. This was all well before Erica got sick. The pediatrician asked how was his vocabulary, how many words does he know.

I repeated the question, stalling. "How many words?" What a strange concept to quantify. I don't know how many words a person knows, or should know at any given time. For the sake of that conversation, it was easier to count the absence of something.

"Not … Um. Barely …"

"Less than a hundred?" he asked. "Fifty? Twenty-five?"

"Um, yeah. Probably that. He mostly grunts when he wants to communicate. 'Ugh, ugh,' and points, like this."

"That isn't good," the pediatrician said.

I was grateful when we switched to another pediatrician. I always left his appointments feeling insecure about Elliot. That morning I felt good about my child's development. By the afternoon I wasn't so sure.

"We should set you up with a speech pathologist right away."

By the time we did get in to see a pathologist, Elliot's speech had developed much more than it had before, and the pathologist said there was nothing to worry about. But one of the things I became aware of was that delayed speech development can be an early indicator of neurodivergence.

Elliot has minor autism. It's been diagnosed only recently, but it was always there. Dyslexia, too.

What does this mean for him? It meant more when he was younger. Especially after Erica died, when he was in a daycare full of strangers, learning how to socialize with children who thought differently than him. I'd pick him up after my work shifts and I could tell which adults in charge understood my child and which ones had no patience for his nonsense. There was a combative quality sometimes, where the daycare administration would approach me about Elliot's unusual traits. How sometimes he wouldn't socialize, he'd just observe other kids playing, as if trying to figure them out. It didn't seem so abnormal to me. I didn't know what the staff's problem was half the time.

Things improved when we changed schools. Still, he had trouble adapting, trouble staying focused. He'd be unable to sit still, or to keep from interrupting the class. Teachers would try to find a way to keep him distracted but still attentive. Fidget devices. Chairs that allowed him to wobble. He was stimming, working through his thoughts physically, and the school staff figured out a way to adapt.

It affected his reading and writing significantly. He has trouble recognizing words committed to paper, and when he speaks, he often trails off in search of the correct word. He comprehends things just fine. I read to the boys every night before bed. Age-appropriate books like YA novels and things of that nature, and he doesn't miss a step. But he struggles sounding out words. And his writing can be chaotic. If you didn't know he was neurodivergent, you might mistake it for unhinged scrawls from a lunatic. Thankfully, we live in an age of text-to-speech technology, and he has apps to help him through these struggles.

Seeing him struggle with reading has certainly humbled me on my attitudes. When the kids were born, I used to say that my only two criteria in raising them were that they be well-read and that they be kind. I guess being well-read will look a little different than how I expected it to look.

I think about when I was in school. We would arrange our desks in a circle, and we'd all read from the same book together, each with our own individual copies but taking turns reading a section out loud. I was always good at sight-reading. It's always come natural to me that when I read words I can instantly say them out loud without tripping over them, or at least without much difficulty. This isn't a natural talent for everyone. In school, when I'd hear the other kids read with effort, sounding out each word with difficulty, I'd think they were the dumbest people alive. I couldn't appreciate how much those children were dreading their turns, knowing they would struggle with this difficult task of reading aloud, knowing their peers would be judging them for it.

Well, that's my kid now. He's the one that's got to struggle through that. Maybe it's my fault for having been arrogant about it all those years ago. Maybe I caused it.

We're constantly shifting the goal posts. Maybe traditional schooling won't give him what he needs. He's got other strengths. Artistic strengths.

At ten he's an excellent drawer and painter, but he is especially good with textiles. He knows how to create stuffed animals from scratch, using Erica's leftover fabric and stuffing we've harvested from lousy pillows. He often makes them just to sell them for cheap, and he's tickled at the idea of his paintings or stuffed animals living at some stranger's house. He's started making a tidy profit, at least for a ten-year-old without an allowance.

Something about the diagnosis kickstarted something in me. I'm not so concerned with him following conventional paths, because I know those paths will never suit him. It's a reminder that we should all do that.

That's what I need in my life. I need an unconventional path.

∘ ∘ ∘ ∘ ∘ ∘ ∘ ∘

SOON, I'D BE going back to Chile for the first time in almost thirty years. I have a conflicted history with the place.

When my parents escaped from there during turmoil in the 1970s, they left a piece of themselves somewhere along the coast.

I visited three times as a child. When I was two, again when I was seven, and finally when I was twelve. The trip at seven was when my dad stayed behind, and the one at twelve was when he broke my heart again. My mom and Julio have a house there that they live in for part of the winter. They were there when Erica died. They said goodbye to her before their trip, fully expecting her to be around and in good health when they returned, but they'd barely just arrived there when Erica went into hospice care and died. I guess we were all in denial about how bad her situation had become. My parents weighed their options and stayed there for the planned duration of their trip.

I resented their decision to stay for quite a while. I refused to see their reasons for staying in Chile and not coming home, which included the fact that they had taken my niece along with them and they owed it to her to see the trip through. When they came back months later, they were showing us photos of the trip. I looked at these pictures of beachfronts and of clear blue oceans, thinking about what had been going on in my life while they'd been on their excursion. I left the viewing and went to sit outside alone.

It took a long time for me to forgive my mom for being gone during that time. I get it now. But my feelings at the time were all about me and what I was going through.

What essentially happened was that I began to compartmentalize a lot of my feelings of abandonment into Chile. Just packed it up and shipped it to a country I never planned on returning to. Fuck it, if an earthquake rips the country to shreds and drops it in the ocean, so be it. My toxic emotions would still be safe there, even at the bottom of the Pacific.

But after Covid-19 subsided and my mom wanted to get back to travelling, she offered to take us back there. We'd be going soon. The idea of going back opened old insecurities in me.

° ° ° ° ° ° ° °

AT A RECENT Christmas, when Charlie was six, Santa brought him a plush fox. Charlie named it Gonzalo. He told me, in front of everyone, "I named it after you because I love you."

"Thanks, bud," I told him. Not for the sentiment.

Thanks for making me look good.

A few weeks later, he came to me in the night worried about the future. That's how he phrased it: "worried about the future." He was concerned about something happening to me. Some tragedy befalling his poor widowed father. I held him while he sobbed, and I could see it hitting him at once, the knowledge that, like his mother, his father would one day die.

I wanted to reassure him with platitudes, tell him nothing would happen to me, that I would stick around for a long time. But I couldn't. I said what I needed to to comfort him in the moment. It would be unfair to suggest I have any power over death. I'm not wily enough to cheat it.

If we had the ability to cheat death, that would mean his mother could have escaped it if she'd really tried. She'd still be here, with her kids, with me, if she'd only wanted it badly enough.

∘ ∘ ∘ ∘ ∘ ∘ ∘ ∘ ∘ ∘

PEOPLE SUGGEST SHE'S in heaven. Which sounds nice. I certainly don't think she'd have been destined for hell. But as I've gotten older, the concept of heaven has lost some of its seductiveness.

Sure, there was a time after Erica's death when I'd look to the skies for guidance, or to utter my thoughts and feelings. Maybe she had pull and could score us some luck. Even though her grandmother's death did nothing to help Erica, I still believed in guardian angels. I get it. It's comforting.

What else is faith but the intersection of what comforts you and what you choose to believe in? For a time I took comfort in heaven and chose to believe in it.

But it's changed.

I can't have a dead person out there worrying over us, fretting, but unable to participate. I wouldn't want that for me.

When I die, I want to be done. A white light. Clean slate. No memories, no imprints. My energy hurtling through the cosmos, broken into immeasurable particles, and then reassembled at the birth of some new life.

I've spent a long time worrying about my kids. I want to be done worrying. I'm sorry they'll be sad when I go, and it's too bad I won't be there to comfort them.

But when I'm gone, I'm done worrying.

Sorry, guys.

° ° ° ° ° ° ° °

THERE HAVE BEEN relationships since. It hasn't been a years-long stretch of bleak mourning. There's been lightness and joy. I've said "I love you" to a few women since Erica died, and I've meant it every time. Those relationships ran their course, ended in a new type of heartache that I was unaccustomed to. Even though it was over, we could still talk. There can be a sadness in that.

In each case I tried to protect the kids. I didn't want them to feel the sting of loss if any of my relationships should end. It happened a few times. Someone was in my life, then they weren't, and the kids became collateral.

Just like their mom was in their life, and now she's not.

I would hate for them to see that as a relationship's natural trajectory, that they were made for ending. That the women in our lives will leave us. I don't want my kids to grow into being the kinds of men who believe that.

So, what can I do about it? The way I see it, it's important they see me in healthy relationships. It's important they see me optimistic in my relationships. Not like I'm parading every first date through their lives, insisting that this person will be their new mom. Nothing like that. But when I'm seeing someone, and they know I'm seeing that someone, I need to commit to it wholeheartedly.

Because I'm proud of my relationships. I'm proud of how I treat the people in my life.

Mostly, as least.

And I want the kids to see that side of me. That relationship side. All they get is the stern, worried, sometimes-affectionate side. But it's not enough. It's only a part of who I am. They're older now, and they deserve to see me for who I really am.

∘ ∘ ∘ ∘ ∘ ∘ ∘ ∘ ∘

ERICA AND I had gotten a cat together when we moved into our first apartment. I didn't even want a cat. We'd just moved into a new place and the last thing I wanted was to be responsible for something. But she was adamant, so we got one. It was a little white ball of fluff that you could fit in the palm of your hand. Her name was Abbey, and yeah, I came to love her pretty quickly.

She moved with us from that first apartment to a second apartment, flew with us to Montreal, then road-tripped back to Winnipeg into temporary homes until we moved into our house. She could be a feisty little demon, but every time we moved, she'd chill out just a little bit more. But even in her docile older years, people visiting stopped trying to pet her because they didn't want their arms and legs ripped to shreds again.

Anyway.

We recently had to put her down.

I've seen it happen before with other pets. Someone comes to the house, to a room where the animal is comfortable.

They administer a sedative to settle it to sleep and then give it a second injection to stop its heart.

It was her back legs. They'd given out. She would drag herself to her water dish and completely ignore her food dish. In her healthy days, when you pet her you'd feel solid meaty flanks of muscle and flesh, but toward the end you'd feel bones through the skin. She'd urinate where she lay, and it would soak into her fur, which she stopped grooming.

Making the decision to have her euthanized began an early grieving process. Charlie would cry at the thought of it. He'd say things like, "She'll always be here in our hearts," which is a touching platitude from a six-year-old, if a little strange. He never even liked the cat all that much. She was around since before his birth, so she was like a piece of furniture, but one that scratched him sometimes. I think he just didn't know what happens when we die, and he was being forced to confront that feeling. He knew the house would feel empty without her.

I recognized that feeling of grieving someone who hasn't died yet. Of sensing what's coming, and, in a sad way, looking forward to it being over so that you yourself can heal.

It was tough to make the decision. She'd still purr when I pet her. I'd think, "How bad can it be, if she still manages to purr?" But I realized she only purred when she was being petted. At least she could do that much. If we were lucky, she would go out purring. Was there a greater gift I could give her? To end her suffering while she was purring? We should all be so lucky to go out that way.

When I first made the decision, I sobbed over her while her chest lifted and lowered with each breath. I thought back to when she was younger. There was a basement apartment that we'd lived in, in a hundred-year-old building. The hallway carpets might not have been as old as the rest of the building, but they sure were very old, and they'd amassed all manner of smells that were exotic to a cat. Whenever I'd open the door to our apartment, Abbey would dart into the hallway so she could sniff the carpets and purr and brush her fur against the walls. I would stick my toes out toward her and she'd bump her face into them, purring and sniffing. I hope wherever she went after this life, it's somewhere that smells like that hallway.

I sobbed for the cat because I was grieving her impending death, but I was also grieving the life we had, when we were young, and my wife was alive. Back then, we only had a cat to depend on us.

When Erica died, I resented the cat for a time. Who was she to live when my wife didn't? That wasn't meant to be the order of things. We got this cat in our first apartment together, and never was she meant to outlive either one of us.

But there's a relief now too. Her death helped me process Erica's death in a way I couldn't before. I prepared for Abbey's burial before she was scheduled to be put down. I dug a deep hole in the backyard, too deep for critters to root out.

When it happened, a man from the veterinary hospital came to my house. I lay down next to Abbey, who was sleeping on a bed of old, clean towels. I had instructed the man to wait for me to call him, because I wanted Abbey purring when he did it. Gentle music played. When Abbey got to purring, I called the man in, and it was like I remembered. One injection to get her to sleep, one more to euthanize her.

After the man left, and I had finished crying for the moment, I carried Abbey outside to the hole in the backyard. I put a thin layer of dirt atop her. Then I added some of Erica's ashes that I still hadn't scattered. More dirt. Then compost, and some grass seeds. That spot of lawn was always notoriously bald from being out of the sunlight.

But you know what?

The grass started to grow. Lush and green, and full of life.

Absolutely beautiful.

∘ ∘ ∘ ∘ ∘ ∘ ∘ ∘ ∘

I STARTED TO think about that old Ouija board that may have hexed my life. I'm sure it didn't, but why shouldn't I hedge my bets? I could use the cleansing anyway.

So I saw psychics. I took salt baths, and hung pepper plants at the edge of my back yard. I filled a jar with old screws and fingernail clippings and buried it somewhere deep. I lined my windowsills with colourful stones, and I started leaving a deck of tarot cards to charge in the moonlight.

I don't know if it's working, but I certainly don't fear having been hexed. Not anymore.

If it was a hex, I sure hope it's over now.

∘ ∘ ∘ ∘ ∘ ∘ ∘ ∘ ∘

THIS LAST WINTER, when Elliot was ten and Charlie seven, we travelled to Chile with my parents for three weeks — me and the kids, my mom and Julio. From my experience with the country, I expected some emotional tragedy to befall us. Some awful event that would make me lose faith in this country. One of the kids getting sucked under the Pacific's rip current, or losing a leg in some wild car accident.

We booked an excursion to an observatory up in the mountains, our small bus winding precarious switchbacks a mile above sea level. I checked our seatbelts obsessively, in case our driver lost control and we careened off the mountainside. Our ears popped from the altitude.

But we didn't tumble over. We saw stars brighter than we'd ever witnessed before. We stood beneath the Southern Cross, and looked at the cluster around Alpha Centauri through a telescope under a domed roof.

We crossed roads, and jumped into the salty ocean whitecaps.

While we were there, the anniversary of Erica's death date came and went. Of course I remembered it. We all did. Seven years. My mom lit a candle in her honour, and friends messaged me to check in. Maybe I was a bit moodier than usual, a bit cloudier. I don't know. After the kids went to sleep I filled my backpack with beers and wandered the neighbourhood, listening to songs she liked, songs I liked, coming to peace with this place and where I was. Where my heart was.

They say that after seven years, our cells have undergone so much natural regeneration that we're no longer even the same people anymore. I do feel changed, but also not. I feel more like the person I used to be before all this happened. As if, in these seven years, my body learned to be more like itself again.

∘ ∘ ∘ ∘ ∘ ∘ ∘ ∘ ∘

AT LAST I loaded the car with the rest of Erica's ashes and headed east into Ontario to Rushing River, the place where I proposed. Whether she still needed me to do it or not, there I stood at the waterline, up to my ankles in cold river current. What mattered was that I needed to do this. Her remains had been in my basement long enough. It was time to let her go.

I opened the bag inside the box and scooped handfuls of ashes into the water until the bag was nothing more than plastic that was dusty with granules. Her remains mingled with the sand and with our memories of the place until they all became the same.

I cried, relieved that it was finally done. But it didn't feel how I'd expected, like I'd let go of some heavy burden. Of course not. It had been years. Much of that burden had been shed away slowly over the years, layer by layer. It would never come off completely, but, after this long, would I even want that feeling to be gone completely? The weight sometimes gives me meaning. I don't know who I would be without it.

° ° ° ° ° ° ° ° °

THE OTHER DAY I was buying cat food from the grocery store. We have a new cat now. The woman running the checkout was telling me about her cat, with a note of sadness in her voice.

"I lost my cat two years ago," she said. I didn't understand immediately that her cat had died and wasn't simply misplaced.

"I'm very sorry to hear that," I told her, and that was true.

"March nineteenth," she said.

"No kidding," I marvelled, thinking about the day Erica died. "I've also had a bad March nineteenth."

Her gaze wandered past me for a moment. "It was so sad," she said. "I still remember." She trailed off for a moment. We'd triggered some memory in her and she had to remember she was at work. "What was your March nineteenth?"

It seemed rude to make things worse. "Oh. We don't need to talk about that."

o o o o o o o o o

I THINK MORE and more about leaving this house.

There's a lot to like about it. It's still home. The neighbourhood is loaded with other kids that are Elliot's and Charlie's ages. Charlie shared a kindergarten class with five kids on our street alone. There's a potential for some of those lifelong bonds you hope to have. Friends who've known you forever.

But it's feeling small. The basement is hollowed stone. It's basically chiselled away, so it looks like a dungeon. We can't use it for a den or a living space. The basement walls are designed to take in water, so building walls that could rot is not advised. It's really just a storage space with a threatening aura.

Elliot has been asking for his own room. The only room I can offer him is my office, which is where I work while they're at school. Of course I'll give it up for him, but I'm not thrilled that I'm being muscled out.

So I've been shopping around for houses on the market. I've got my eye on a neighbourhood I like. Someplace big enough for us. Bigger. I want more people in my life.

We'd need two bathrooms.

We'd be leaving behind some fruit trees that I planted. But I could plant more at the new place.

I'd have reason to get rid of so much clutter. Things I just don't want anymore but can't bring myself to clean. I'd certainly be more motivated to make space.

A fresh start. Gosh, could a thing like that even be possible?

∘ ∘ ∘ ∘ ∘ ∘ ∘ ∘

DURING THE SUMMER, four months after Erica died, we packed up the car for a camping trip with some close friends. They handled the arrangements for us: bringing the food, booking the site, you name it. We were only in charge of our tent and our snacks.

I felt confident because I'd been going through something of a calm spell. I knew these spells were something of a self-delusion. I'd go six days maybe without a tantrum, or eight, or twelve. It didn't matter. There was always a ticking clock inching us toward the next blowout. Acknowledging the calm spell always seemed to trigger the next great reset. "Holy hell," I'd tell myself, "we're doing pretty well." And by thinking it, the countdown timer would begin, and within seventy-two hours, some inanimate object in the house would get bashed to smithereens, and the kids would add to their repertoire of colourful swear words.

On this July morning, loading up the car for our trip, I thought to myself, *This is a good time for a camping trip. My nerves have rarely been better.* I popped the kids in front of the television so I could make all the necessary trips to the car. Charlie was only a year old then, so he would have been strapped to a chair of sorts, or secured in a playpen. I fed the cat and triple-checked that the doors were locked. Then I stuffed the kids into their car seats and built a fort around them with blankets and pillows. They had snacks and stuffies galore. I had my music, and the directions scrawled onto some scrap paper. The trip was an estimated two and a half hours, which was a dicey length by at least an hour. I didn't know if the kids could make that trip easily. But hey, we were having a calm spell.

Three hours later, and we were completely lost. Elliot kept asking how long it would be until we were there. He did so at different volumes and pitches, sometimes conversationally, sometimes as a song. "When will we get there? When will we get therrrre?" Charlie whined in his seat. No amount of soothers or formula or arrowroot cookies would quiet him down. We were inching along a winding forest road, and I was terrified that every blind turn would result in a head-on collision. Pickup trucks rode my tailgate and I would wave them past. I kept telling the kids, "Just to the end of this road, guys, just to the end," but I didn't know if that was true, because I didn't know where we were or where we were going. At last we exited the forest and came to a clearing that immediately looped into a dead end. There was only lake water around us. No campsites. My phone wasn't helping me. I waited for a map to load, and when it did load it told me nothing of value. My friends were at the site, and they either had no signal or weren't answering my calls, so I left them frantic, sobbing voicemails that they'd hear later when they were back in the city. We returned the way we came, back down the hairy forest road. I played calming music over the stereo, but my hands were trembling on the steering wheel. I felt a panic attack coming at highway speeds. Charlie wailed and I screamed at him to just stop crying already. That went over as well as could be expected, screaming at a baby to be quiet. I pulled over onto a safe stretch of prairie road and got out of the car. I didn't want to be parked on the shoulder but the road was straight and flat, and I could see the horizon at either end. So I screamed. I shouted for Erica to help me, goddamn it. Why wasn't she here to help me? I stamped my feet like I wanted to break the bones in my heels. I picked up a rock and nearly smashed the car window. Thankfully, I had awareness enough to launch it into the ditch.

If there was a park, I'd have stopped there and found a moment to regroup. Let the boys stretch their legs so that we could start fresh. The kids were eager to be unshackled from their seatbelts and run around, but we didn't have any place here on the highway shoulder to do it.

So we trudged on. Miraculously, we soon came across a sign pointing us in the right direction. We arrived at the site, broken, after nearly four hours in the car. I was a shell of myself.

But then the camping trip did what camping trips do. I felt myself become refreshed and recharged. After so much buildup, we ended up enjoying a great weekend of riding bikes and swimming and playing. The adults there helped me shoulder some responsibility so that I could do things like go to the bathroom without worrying about a toddler every second. I was immensely grateful.

This all occurred during a time that I was choosing to believe Erica was there to answer me when I needed the help. On the way home, the kids mercifully fell asleep before we even reached the highway. Likely, they'd have slept the whole way home if I'd let them. I followed the flow of traffic back toward the city, which took us by an alternate route. It makes sense, since our journey out was such a boondoggle. This route took us through Lockport, a small township just outside the city. Lockport is something of a tourist hub for summertime day trippers looking to escape for a few hours. Erica loved Lockport, and she'd visit it whenever she could. I took this as a sign.

I pulled into a diner parking lot and shook the boys awake. We ate chicken fingers and french fries and blue bubble-gum–flavoured ice cream cones. Elliot and I popped quarters into the arcade machines while Charlie watched us, strapped into his highchair. Next to the diner was a large vacant field running off the highway. I laid Charlie down on the grass and changed his diaper. The kids took off their shoes and played in the grass, pretending to be kites in the breeze. They made me be a rainbow, and I arched my body with my hands and feet touching the ground while they crawled underneath me, as flying kites would. Butterflies danced around us. The smell of the river filled the late afternoon air. We drove the rest of the way home with the windows down.

Acknowledgements

I HAD WANTED to write about Erica since she died. Everything I wrote was terrible. Loose ends, unconnected threads. More than that, I didn't want to think about those awful times, the last days, the days after. There were two children who needed me in the present, and not trapped somewhere in the past. Besides, who was I even writing this for?

On Easter weekend, three years ago, my friend Julie Mannell, who was an acquisitions editor for Dundurn, asked me if I wanted to write a book. I asked her if this was a hypothetical question, and she said no. She knew my writing, and she wanted me to tell my story.

After months of fretting and writing nothing, I quit the project. Julie kept me on track by convincing me that book contracts are ironclad, and getting out of one is hard. Of course I didn't believe her. But she believed in me, and this project, and I owe her my thanks for that.

Thanks also to everyone at Dundurn that I've gotten to work closely with: Susan Fitzgerald and Erin Pinksen and Jess Shulman and Laura Boyle, as well as everybody I haven't yet met.

To my mom and to Julio (Lita and Tata to the kids), for always being there for me. Ditto Laury and Ron, who make sure I can get time to myself as often as I do.

Dozens of friends have been there for me over the years. I mentioned none of them by name in this book, but they know who they are.

And to my kids: I guess I'll see you at breakfast tomorrow.

About the Author

Photo by Duncan McNairnay

GONZALO RIEDEL IS a Winnipeg writer. He lives in a one-hundred-year-old house with his two children, Elliot and Charlie, and their cat, Milkshake. He is terrified of ghosts.